TWAYNE'S WORLD AUTHORS SERIES

A Survey of the World's Literature

SPAIN

Janet W. Díaz, Texas Tech University

EDITOR

Juan Eugenio Hartzenbusch

TWAS 501

Royal Court House in Sevilla (mid. 16th Cent.)

JUAN EUGENIO HARTZENBUSCH

By CARMEN IRANZO

TWAYNE PUBLISHERS

A DIVISION OF G. K. HALL & CO., BOSTON

Published in 1978 by Twayne Publishers,
A Division of G. K. Hall & Co.
All Rights Reserved

Printed on permanent/durable acid-free paper and bound
in the United States of America

First Printing

Library of Congress Cataloging in Publication Data

Iranzo, Carmen.
Juan Eugenio Hartzenbusch.

(Twayne's world authors series ; TWAS 501 : Spain)
Bibliography: p. 145-47
Includes index.
1. Hartzenbusch, Juan Eugenio, 1806-1880—Criticism
and interpretation.
PQ6528.I7   1978   862'.5   78-6878
ISBN 0-8057-6342-2

To Los Amantes de Teruel
And All Those Who Have
an Impossible Love

Contents

About the Author

Carmen Iranzo Campos was born in Valencia, Spain and later moved with her family to Mexico—where her father was living in exile. She has since taught Spanish at Amherst College, the University of Massachusetts, Adelphi University and Hofstra University and is presently living in Chapel Hill, North Carolina where her husband is professor of Spanish Literature.

The author has performed as actress and singer since adolescence and has done considerable research in Spanish vocal music, and, recently, received an award at the Siglo de Oro Festival (held at the Chamizal Theater in El Paso, Texas) for her costumes.

Iranzo has published articles and book reviews in *Hispanófila* as well as short stories in anthologies including: *Insula, Voces de Mañana,* and *Cinco Cuentistas Contemporáneos.* She has also published five books including: a translation of Roberto de Nola's *Libro de Cozina,* an edition of *Los Amantes de Teruel* by Andrés Rey de Artieda and Tirso de Molina, *Agridulce*–a collection of original short stories, an edition of *La Niña de Gómez Arias* by Luis Vélez de Guevara and Pedro Calderón de la Barca, and an edition of Linton Lomas Barret's study of *Como Padre y Como Rey* by Juan Pérez de Montalbán. Currently, the author is working on a book about Antonio García Gutiérrez forthcoming in Twaynes's World Authors Series.

Preface

The author studied in this book occupies a prominent place in Spanish letters. His contributions are manifold, so it is not merely as a writer that he has achieved fame. Juan Eugenio Hartzenbusch tried his hand at being a dramatist, critic, historian, librarian, and was a constant researcher of written works. He possessed a vast knowledge of Spanish and other European theater and knew several languages. All these interests helped him achieve an erudition that earned him fame and admiration among his contemporaries and has kept his name in a privileged position. Spanish children learn his fables in school; students use his editions of seventeenth-century Spanish plays written by some of the foremost dramatists of the times; theater lovers know his name largely by virtue of a single play, which came at the height of the Romantic movement. His judgments on grammar, dictionary entries, and his works in general are esteemed by scholars everywhere.

It is precisely in this connection that I welcome the commission to prepare a book about this author. My views on his achievements differ from the vast majority of people who take Hartzenbusch's work at face value, who see his contribution to the glory of Spanish letters but who overlook or ignore the errors of fact and statement he committed. His good intentions and his unquestionable erudition somehow have blinded many eyes to the flaws and inconsistencies found throughout his works, an aspect that has to be brought to light in order to separate his solid research from the doubtful and inaccurate.

Hartzenbusch had a peculiar point of view. Even when faced with contradictory evidence, he kept his own criteria, in many cases often trying to justify the indefensible if he thought it was harmless. In his effort to revive an interest in the Spanish theater of ages past he did his research in an erratic way. At times he picked on a single line to discuss and prove the lack of ability of the playwright, or to establish chronology, stating as gospel truth what he thought, without checking further. He might not say a word about the historic or legendary origin, but often he tried to establish the precise events that took place at a given point in time, bringing out another playwright's ignorance of such facts, when the author in question merely used the historic as background to develop his plot.

This is particularly annoying when Hartzenbusch himself, basically an unoriginal mind, copied someone else's plays, reworking them in his own way, and wove tales around historic figures, imputing to them doubtful morals. More information on this point will be found in the evaluation and discussion of several plays, such as *Alfonso el Casto, Los Amantes de Teruel,* and others. Often a stickler for detail, at least he should have been more consistently accurate, and not have attributed feet of clay to kings known for their good deeds, since after all it is the way they govern that affects people. The damage done in such instances is comparable to the disservice done today when a classical subject is treated as a musical comedy, killing the impact or distorting the plot to suit the modern adaptation.

The statements and judgments made in this sketchy evaluation will be shown in the following pages in detail, insofar as this type of book allows. If this volume were written in Spanish, I would undertake to clarify every wrong statement made by Hartzenbusch, whether acknowledged in subsequent works or not, as my contribution to setting the record straight to some aspects of the literature of my own country. Here I have to limit myself to bringing out specifically some of the liberties Hartzenbusch took while reworking others' works, and some of the changes he devised. I intend to point out the considerable contribution of Hartzenbusch to the realm of letters and his valuable effort at disseminating them, but with a word of caution. Many notes and quotations lifted directly from his works are inaccurate; this helps perpetuate false information and omissions that merit further research and not mere repetition.

I wish to thank professor Janet Diaz for giving me the opportunity, although unintentionally, to do justice to the subject of the play that catapulted Hartzenbusch to fame, *Los Amantes de Teruel.* I have done considerable research on the historic legend, as it was the theme of my Master of Arts thesis, the subject of a subsequent edition of the first two plays on the legend, and two papers presented at Modern Language Association meetings. [1] In the absence of complete works, our author's production had to be gathered from many sources, which may account for an involuntary omission. Given the large amount and variety of writings, the length of this volume precludes the inclusion of a detailed study of his editions of plays by Fray Gabriel Téllez, (Tirso de Molina), as well as an extensive part of

Preface

Hartzenbusch's notes to the *Quijote*. It is hoped the interested
Hispanist will pursue such study on his own. Also, for reasons of
space, many quotations in Spanish have to be omitted from the notes
and references. The dramatic efforts of our author, preeminent in his
total production, are treated in more detail, while other writings such
as fables, poetry, articles, and short stories have had to be dealt with
in a less extensive manner. Representative contributions in each
genre are examined.

It is hoped that Hispanists, well versed in the particular period of
Hartzenbusch's lifetime, will abide by my desire to explain to those
less familiar with Spanish letters rather elementary information that
is not repetitive for the uninitiated. Avid defenders of our writer will
do well to read, or reread, as the case may be, his works, bearing in
mind my observations. The English translations, unless sanctioned
by use, are my own. This is a thankless task given the dissimilarities
between English and Spanish. Many words and concepts defy translation, and often the literal rendition has to give way to the meaning.

CARMEN IRANZO

Chronology

1806   Born in Madrid on September 6.

1808   His mother dies.

1821   Goes to the theater for the first time.

1823   Begins translating French plays into Spanish.

1828   Makes his own version of classic Spanish plays.

1829   Begins writing his own plays. First play performed in a public theater, *El amo criado* (The Master Servant).

1830   Marries María Morgue on April 23. His father dies on June 3.

1836   His wife dies.

1837   Presents his most important play, *Los Amantes de Teruel,* (The Lovers of Teruel).

1838   Marries Salvadora Hiriart on December 15.

1839   Begins his editions of Spanish classic authors. Performance of *La redoma encantada* (The Enchanted Phial) on October 26.

1840   His son, Eugenio Maximino, is born.

1841   First performance of *Alfonso el Casto,* in June.

1843   Publishes poetic and literary essays.

1844   Holds a high post in the Biblioteca Nacional of Madrid.

1845   First performance of *La Jura en Santa Gadea* (The Swearing at Saint Gadea) on May 29.

1847   Becomes a member of the Royal Spanish Academy.

1848   Publishes fables.

1852   First performance of *Sancho Ortiz de las Roelas.*

1854   First performance of *La Archiduquesita* (The Little Archduchess) November 8.

1855   Director of the Normal School for Elementary Education.

1860   Presents *El mal apóstol y el buen ladrón* (The Bad Apostle and the Good Thief) on February 25.

1862   Becomes director of the Biblioteca Nacional.

1867   His second wife dies.

1875   Retires as director of the Biblioteca Nacional.

1880   Dies on August 2. Performance of his posthumous play *Heliodora o el amor enamorado* (Heliodora or Love in Love) in September.

CHAPTER 1

Life and Works

I Biography

JUAN Eugenio Hartzenbusch was born in Madrid, September 6,
1806. His father, Santiago, left his native village of Schwadorf,
Germany, at age nineteen. He had been a farmer like his father, but
followed his brother Juan to Spain, where he became a carpenter and
furniture maker. There he married María Josefa Martínez Calleja,
daughter of a farmer from Valparaíso de Abajo, in the province of
Cuenca. Scarcely two years after Juan Eugenio was born his mother
gave birth to another boy, dying two weeks later. How the widowed
man and his two little boys managed without her is not mentioned in
any of the biographical material, only that the children seldom saw
anyone, or talked to people other than the workers at the carpentry
shop, and that only during working hours.

His father wanted Juan Eugenio to pursue religious studies, which
the boy did not want to do, so he studied French and Italian, as well as
Greek and Latin, from an old Jesuit priest, and two years of
philosophy in San Isidro el Real in Madrid. He worked at his father's
shop but read plays and continued studying languages. By chance he
read a treatise on metrics and art written by Father Losada. In 1821,
in the absence of the elder Hartzenbusch, who was not interested in
art in any form, the two brothers went to the theater for the first time
in their lives. The experience served to increase the young man's
interest in the theater, and he soon began translating plays from the
French and Italian, adapting others from German and from Spanish
classic authors—some in verse, some in prose—adding and suppres-
sing or altering things in his own way. Some of his early adaptations
were performed in a private home, where he, his brother and a few
friends displayed their potential talents as actors and playwrights.
One of the young actresses became his wife.

These early efforts, the product of his love for the theater but

15

lacking real knowledge of the art of writing for the stage, were less than fortunate, but Hartzenbusch did not seek counsel from anybody nor did he study any of the plays he translated and adapted in their artistic context, a product of someone else's work. This lack of preparation was never corrected. The atmosphere at home, with a taciturn, uninterested father, was certainly not conducive to great things, but Hartzenbusch trusted to his own intellect. Some of his plays performed in private were not printed; the same lot befell some presented in commercial theaters, while others were published but never performed. He also had his share of successful productions, but his peculiar way of writing never changed, so the numerous reworkings of his own plays, whether original or adapted, were not necessarily improvements.

An untiring researcher, totally dedicated to literature, Hartzenbusch also wrote numerous articles on various subjects, from speeches for the Ateneo (Atheneum) of Madrid to dramatic criticism, poetry, and fables (mainly translated and adapted from the German), short stories, introductions to books, obituaries, and dictionary entries. He also edited works of Spanish classic writers and did an annotated edition of the *Quijote*, adding to his notes years later. Meanwhile, Hartzenbusch earned a living at his father's carpentry shop. He married María Morgue in April of 1830, and in June of the same year his father, reduced to idiocy and with only one client left, died.

In 1831 Hartzenbusch was studying shorthand, which earned him a post at the Parliament, taking notes and transcribing speeches. Antonio Ferrer del Río, who worked with him, describes him as mysterious, studious, always on time, wearing a blue cape, with an umbrella if the weather was threatening, well groomed, poorly dressed, uncommunicative. At this time he was under thirty. Ferrer also says Hartzenbusch did not take everything down and eliminated a great deal, but at least he did not add words to those of the politicians. Practicing journalism as well, he moved slowly toward the beloved world of letters. His frail wife died in 1836, before Hartzenbusch enjoyed his biggest success with the presentation of *Los Amantes de Teruel* (The Lovers of Teruel, 1837), which was widely acclaimed by his contemporaries and by many others later. This play, reviewed by Mariano José de Larra, a controversial man very much in the public eye, placed our author immediately at the head of the Romantic playwrights. He found himself able to write and publish anything he wanted.

In 1838 he married for the second time. His wife was Salvadora Hiriart, a widow, born in Bayonne, daughter of Juan Hiriart and Catalina Manzanares, from Sepúlveda, province of Segovia. Her first husband, José Vercruysse, from Courtray, Belgium, had died in 1834. Salvadora, eight years older than Juan Eugenio, brought to the marriage five children, the oldest a girl of twenty; two more children had died. Hartzenbusch received all of them well and seemingly had a good family life. His only son, Salvadora's eighth, was born in 1840. He did not marry.

More plays of varying success followed, as well as literary essays and poems. In 1844 he was a high official at the Biblioteca Nacional of Madrid (National Library), an enviable job for one so inclined to erudition. By then Hartzenbusch was able to obtain much necessary material for his editions and playwriting. In 1847 he was made a member of the Royal Spanish Academy; later, in 1855, he became director of the Normal School for Elementary Education, after having published a collection of fables. The culmination of his academic life came in 1862, when at the death of his good friend Agustín Durán, Hartzenbusch replaced him as Director of the Biblioteca Nacional. His complaint about the new post was lack of time, and of peace and quiet to work on his own writings.

Emilio Castelar, one of the greatest orators Spain has known, describes him in his old age as thin, of ruddy complexion and whitish hair; short, myopic, alert, nervous, of simple habits, pleasant but hesitating at the start of a conversation, although vivacious at the end; cautious about revealing personal achievements, but warming up to friends in the long run, humble and sensitive, of lofty thought and strong will. The death of his second wife in 1867 greatly affected Hartzenbusch, but he managed to continue working and doing research until retirement in 1875. His last piece of work was dated and published in 1874. He died in Madrid, August 2, 1880.

II *The Romantic Period in Spain as it Relates to Hartzenbusch*

The Romantic period is too well known to need even an elementary description. A product of the 1800s, due to many causes, its political and artistic aspects were by far the best known. Perhaps it is a little simplistic to try to link the repressive government of King Ferdinand VII to whatever was printed at the time, from newspaper articles to poems, from dramatic pieces to novels, thus trying to establish a trend of collective thinking which could not exist. The most effect governmental rules and edicts might have would be that of censorship, a word and concept that automatically promotes a reaction of mistrust, rebellion, and protest. In an epoch when so many plays were based on legends and historic events, building on a dissenting note could be variously construed by the regime's critic of the moment. The theory common among foreigners and Spanish Francophiles, that what makes the Romantic movement different in Spain is its supposed importation from France by returning exiles, is counterbalanced by the facts, and is stated by many scholars and public figures.

Many plots and countless elements and ideas used in the elaboration of Romantic plays, be they French, German, or Italian operas, came directly from Spanish sources. The main foreign element that dominated the artistic expressions of the period was the Italian music, brought to Spain by the Bourbons. Eduardo Rincón, in his prologue to Antonio Peña y Goñi's *La opera española y la música dramática en España en el siglo XIX*,[1] (The Spanish Opera and Dramatic Music in Spain in the XIX Century) states that Spanish musicians, instead of opposing the Italian opera and working to displace it, let it thrive along with their own music and even copied it. He also points out that Spaniards disregarded their recent history and, rejecting the models left by the times of Goya and his paintings, looked at other historic times.

Peña y Goñi observes that the Italians may have been in Spain playing their music, but at the same time there were Spanish musicians scattered all over Europe, as the case had been since the fifteenth century. Spanish singers were preferred then to the Italian and Flemish for the Pope's chapel, and they left their mark, influencing Italian music. There were other Spanish musicians in Bologna; their music was published in Rome and Venice; Juan Tapia, the founder of the first conservatory of music in Naples, was a Spaniard; Juan del Encina was the organist and composer for Pope Leo X; Bartolomé Ramos Pareja, Tomás Luis de Victoria, Cristóbal Morales, and many others taught, performed, and left a considerable imprint wherever they went; Francisco Soto de Langa and St. Philip Neri created the oratorio form. These are but a few examples. Another observation made by Peña y Goñi is that inspiration and study may produce a more or less well-constructed composition, but the flavor and special national characteristics that reflect a country in its music cannot be improvised. Consistency and tradition eventually produce such things as a national opera.

The same can be said in the case of the musical expressions of Spain in the Romantic period: the sporadic use of music in the theater of the Golden Age by Lope de Vega, Tirso, Calderón, Cervantes, and many others, the lyric compositions of Juan del Encina, and early musical pieces labeled as operas or *zarzuelas* (similar to musical comedy with alternating singing and dialogue) were the seed. The wealth of songs found in the many extant collections and the several types of plays using music did not produce a theatrical work with a national profile until the modern *zarzuela* came into being. Whether or not it was influenced by the Italian element, the *zarzuela* is unmistakably Spanish. According to Antonio Peña y Goñi Queen Cristina, fourth wife of Ferdinand VII, created the Madrid conservatory at the height of the popularity of Italian music (especially Rossini's operas), and instead of giving the post to a Spaniard she named the Italian Piermarini head of the new institution. Since this study is not of music but of the work of Hartzenbusch, suffice it to say that music for the theater was very much in vogue, especially the Italian, which in turn was heavily influenced by the Spanish for several centuries.

In the world of letters there has been much discussion about what is a Romantic Play, what aims and goals authors in each country were pursuing. The break with Neoclassicism may have been a rebellion against rule, political and intellectual, but there had to be a new product, of raw materials from the existing mines. It was no longer enough to present lofty ideas or everyday happenings; the individual had to be taken into consideration also, as a living creature, not fictitious. What could be better than portraying real feelings and private tragedies wrought into an intricate pattern whose design was as rich as heavy embroidery, thick with underlying stitches that added bulk and confusion?

Turning toward the individual could only result in as many stories as there are human feelings, in different contexts, and using historic figures and times was one way of doing this. Precisely because human feelings have been in the world since its creation, the stories of ancient heroes, wars, treason, the burdens of kings and other rulers, repeat themselves with variations in each case. Adding the personal element, usually missing when dealing with a specific episode in the life of a prominent person, making emotion the focal point, had met with the disapproval of earlier critics, as shown by their defense of the restrictions of the stage to gods, kings, and noblemen and having the story take place in an uninterrupted period of time. Birth, death, a ceremony, a physical mishap, take only a moment; the events that lead to them do not. Depicting a battle onstage calls for endless messengers or secondary characters to bring news constantly; a dilemma that has to be resolved requires the protagonists to supply the necessary background through dialogue. All that had been disregarded for many years in the Spanish theater.

If it is true that legends found in the folklore of many countries were revived, Spain was very much in the lead. Those plays that gave prominence to their authors, either through popular or critical acclaim, were preceeded by many that were less fortunate. Such is the case with Hartzenbusch until he wrote *Los Amantes de Teruel* (The Lovers of Teruel). Whatever its beauties and defects, it made an impact as did Antonio García Gutiérrez's *El Trovador* (The Troubadour) and Victor Hugo's *Hernani.* All three themes were Spanish, and in the case of the latter two, their fame did not stop there: Giuseppe Verdi found them worthy of his inspired music, as well as many other plays by Spaniards or with Spanish themes.[2]

These brief examples point up the fact that a movement such as Romanticism could not be "imported" by a country already doing what the Romantics were discovering. If there had been early Romantic figures such as Werther, and novels and short stories that lent themselves to Romantic form in the theater, the fact of their being written works made their coming to life very complex, having to adapt to a different medium with exacting needs.

Pedro Calderón de la Barca is usually credited with having done, in the seventeenth century, what the Romantics were putting in practice, and with being a rich source for Romantic themes. The same can be said of other Golden Age Spanish writers and dramatists and this tradition, aside from foreign themes and adaptations, was the main and inexhaustible spring for Spanish writers. Juan Alcina Franch attributes to an evolutionary movement away from Neoclassicism, prior to the domination of the so-called French school of Romanticism, the desire of the Spanish audiences to see onstage conflicts as they were, close to reality, not curbed forever by obedience, sense of duty, and social conventions. Thus authors put their protagonists in extreme situations, stretching the action (as opposed to long speeches) in a somewhat morbid manner.

The exaggeration of having not only a dramatic situation resulting in a tragic ending for one or more of the characters, but literally living some aspects of the protagonist's state of mind and mood in a physical way is masterfully described by Ramón de Mesonero Romanos in his *Escenas matritenses* (Madrid Scenes, 1837). A young man, unwashed, with long hair, dreamy eyes, "fateful forehead," pale cheeks barely seen through the brush in his unkempt beard, linked to his mustache, and sideburns, wears tight pants, a shorter than normal jacket buttoned up to the neck, a black scarf sloppily tied, and a hat of mysterious shape, forced to rest on his left eyebrow; altogether, he is sinister-looking and so sullen that it is difficult to tell his front from his back. Mesonero depicts a play, an imaginary one written by the young man just described, as being "a Romantic Natural Drama, emblematic-subliminal, anonymous, synonymous, tetric and spasmodic, original, in diverse prose and verse meters, in six acts and fourteen parts" and set "in the 4th and 5th centuries. The locale is all of Europe and the action lasts about one hundred years."

Eugenio de Tapia, in *El Café* (The Café, 1832), makes light of a fictitious, hopeful poet who says:

> I have among my dirty manuscripts
> an original drama of great invective
> in six acts, where ten people talk,
> and I kill five of them, and I reduce a city
> to ashes, raining thunderbolts,
> and fearsomely the sea growls and shakes;
> but after the furor of the storm
> the morning star appears,
> and from it, flying fast, descends
> a deity announcing marvels,
> and the curtain falls. How much applause
> will come upon me (if they don't boo it!).

Judging by the many accounts of what Romanticism was, one might be led to believe that men stood in the street, airing their political views, their intellectual and sentimental state, or, as an alternative, living the part and writing about it in periodicals. Perhaps not many people could escape being affected in some measure by the complex array of things making up the times. The concept of Romanticism from the recent yet advantageous viewpoint of 1885 was expressed by Antonio Cánovas del Castillo, head of the Spanish government, in his prologue to Pedro de Novo y Colson's *Autores dramáticos contemporáneos y joyas del teatro español del siglo XIX* (Contemporary Dramatic Authors and Jewels of the XIX Century Spanish Theater, 1881), in these terms: The world of Calderón ended with his century, and that of Ramón de la Cruz with his, the eighteenth; he filled his plays with vanishing types; the theater of Moratín lacked poetry, but that was a product of the times. Lyricism came after many translations of bad plays had been staged along with a few mediocre Spanish ones. Fill a theater today, Cánovas says, not with critics and rich people, not with intellectuals, philosophers, or those who only bother with the cosmopolitan life, but with every day run-of-the-mill people, workers, and show them any play by the Duke of Rivas, García Gutiérrez, Hartzenbusch's *Los Amantes de Teruel* (The Lovers of Teruel), Zorrilla's plays, and you will see true emotion. What these people applaud is the poetry, the same lyric Spanish element that shone in the dramas and comedies of old. Don't look for psychological studies or analyses of the human soul; the splendid poetry is what makes them triumph.

The times seek a unity of thought and universal life that is utopian and far off; nations are still different and will preserve their historic character, especially those that have not advanced or declined somewhat, as was the case with Spain, where the reign of Charles V and the teachings of Don Quijote still seem very much alive. This sense of history is the element that explains modern theater; no matter how some try to follow other trends, the taste runs to the dramatic works with reminiscences of the past.

Cánovas quotes Luis Morales de Polo, who two centuries before raised the question of what fixed rules of art are found in dramatic works, arguing that even if one admits that Aristotle and Plato claimed them to exist, who has followed them in Spain? There the *comedia* has the majesty and splendor of the epic poem, the delights of the lyric; fables have a bit of historic truth; real episodes have the somberness of tragedy, the wit and fun of light comedy, the spicy element of satire, all in moderation. He offers Victor Hugo's *Hernani* as contrast, where these elements are found, but in an unfortunate combination.

What can be concluded from this sketchy picture of the Romantic period in Spain is that those elements that made it a movement were present, passively or actively, and foreign products were received in ways ranging from total rejection to all-out imitation. Hartzenbusch was affected by the intellectual climate of the country, the urge to write, do research, foster his lyric and erudite inclinations, and his love for scholarly endeavors in general. In many different ways, admiring and imitating the foreign and national literature and dramatic works, he aired his views in periodicals, speeches, fables, articles, and above all in his writings for the theater. Let us see the marks he left.

III *Résumé of Works*

The chronology of production is hard to follow because Hartzenbusch did more than one thing at the same time, including revisions of his own plays. Of utmost importance is a bibliography compiled by his son, Eugenio Maximino.[3] According to his catalogue of works, published in 1900, several plays were never printed, although some of these were performed, either in a conventional or private theater. Other works underwent more than one revision or adaptation, but it is not clear whether such retouchings reached the theater audiences or were confined to the printed page only.

There is no edition of Hartzenbusch's complete works; it would be a challenging task, given the amount of unpublished plays, translations, free adaptations, imitations, works written in collaboration with others, articles scattered through newspapers and magazines, as well as prologues and speeches. Practically every word he ever wrote has been preserved by his son. The reader is therefore referred to this source of information (sometimes inaccurate) for a detailed account of our author's production. Even the more complete anthologies repeat his most successful plays with varying revisions, a circumstance that makes it impossible to detail briefly and accurately the specific nature of his writings. In the case of translations, adaptations, imitations, and the like, one would need to read the original play, preferably in the language in which it was written, to ascertain the changes made by Hartzenbusch, since his acknowledgment of sources varies from extensive notes to not a word. Not being of utmost importance, only some representative adaptations will be treated at length. Plays that caused controversy, were successful on stage, or that show their author's drive to try his hand on a given subject already treated by somebody else will be discussed.

The most important collections to be dealt with in the corresponding sections are: *Teatro escogido de Fray Gabriel Téllez. conocido con el nombre de El Maestro Tirso de Molina* (Selected Theater by Friar Gabriel Téllez, known by the name of Master Tirso de Molina). Tomos I–XII. Madrid, Yenes, 1839–42. *Ensayos poéticos y artículos en prosa, literarios y de costumbres* (Poetic Essays and Prose, Literary and Costumbristic Articles). Madrid, Yenes, 1843. This book contains twenty poems, thirty fables adapted from Lessing, four articles of literary criticism, and eleven Costumbristic articles which resemble short stories. *Comedias de Don Pedro Calderón de la Barca* (Plays of Pedro Calderón de la Barca), I–IV. Biblioteca de Autores

Españoles. Tomos VII, IX, XII, XIV. Madrid, 1848–50; *Obras escogidas de don J. E. Hartzenbusch* (Selected Works of J. E. Hartzenbusch). Paris, Baudry, 1850. Containing the latest revisions made by the author, it has a prologue by Eugenio de Ochoa, although only his initials appear at the end of it. Since the plays and other writings are found elsewhere, and a study of them is made in this book, only the preliminary text is important in this instance. *Comedias de Fray Gabriel Téllez (El Maestro Tirso de Molina), juntas en colección e ilustradas por D. Juan Eugenio Hartzenbusch* (Selected Plays by Friar Gabriel Téllez [Master Tirso de Molina], Collected in an Anthology and Illustrated), B.A.E.,V. Madrid, 1848; 2a edición 1850. To date I have not been able to find any edition bearing the 1848 date. *Comedias de Don Juan Ruiz de Alarcón y Mendoza* (Plays of Juan Ruiz de Alarcón y Mendoza). B.A.E. Tono XX. Madrid, Rivadeneyra, 1852; *Comedias escogidas de Fray Lope Félix de Vega Carpio* (Selected Plays by Friar Lope Félix de Vega Carpio), B.A.E., I–IV, XXIV, XXXIV, XLI, XLII. Madrid, 1835–57; *Obras escogidas*. Edición alemana dirigida por el autor (Selected Works, German Edition Directed by the Author), Leipzig, Brockhaus, 1863. With a prologue by Antonio Ferrer del Río, the two volumes bound together contain: the first nine tales, old vocabulary, fifty fables, twelve poems, and two plays. The second volume contains five plays. *El Ingenioso Hidalgo Don Quijote de la Mancha* (The Ingenious Knight Don Quijote de la Mancha), by Miguel de Cervantes Saavedra, I–IV. Argamasilla de Alba, Rivadeneyra, 1863: *Las 1.633 notas puestas por el Excmo. é ilmo. señor D. Juan Eugenio Hartzenbusch á la primera edición de "El ingenioso hidalgo,"* reproducida por D. Francisco López Fabra con la fototipia (The 1,633 notes to the first edition of the *Quijote*) Barcelona, Ramírez y Cía, 1874. The notes to the *Quijote* appear in assorted publications of the times, greatly differing in number. For this reason the four-volume edition Hartzenbusch made of the novel, as well as the 1,633 notes he published in 1874, will be discussed in this book. Other collections mentioned by Hartzenbusch's son repeat much of the contents of the previously listed anthologies, with variations as to versions of a given play. Articles and prologues are scattered in different publications, such as *El Español, La Iberia, La Constitución, Revista de Europa, El Heraldo, La Gaceta de Madrid, Revista de Teatros, Las Novedades, Semanario Pintoresco Español, Los Niños, El Corresponsal, El Laberinto, El Entreacto,* and *Revista de España y del Extranjero.*

Given the array of pieces of different lengths touching many subjects, for the sake of clarity the divisions will be generic, in chronological order within each classification, if known. As the largest portion of Hartzenbusch's production is theater, that part will of necessity be longer than the others.

CHAPTER 2

Compositions for the Theater

E UGENIO Maximino Hartzenbusch zealously included in his catalogue any and all titles by his father that he found, whether printed or scribbled on a piece of paper. As many of them are free adaptations and others are unavailable, not every title is recorded here. It seems best to group Hartzenbusch's dramatic works by types or approximate categories, for the sake of clarity, and give preference to those plays that are not translations.

A dramatic work is wrought to be performed on stage, not simply to be read; that is the function of novels and poetry. The reader who doesn't even imagine a play being acted is missing the point entirely; it is worse still when the playwright himself thinks of his work that way. Thus, in many plays by Hartzenbusch there are unresolved situations, a profusion of distracting elements that add nothing, and a lack of information vital to follow the thread. Sometimes interest is aroused, but diluted as the author disperses his characters in too many directions. These things have to do with a misplaced dramatic sense on the part of the author; he knows what he wants to say, but especially in an historic play there are incidents or facts that should at least be brought up; the danger is precisely there, in bringing out so many items that are irrelevant to the plot.

In his peculiar way of discerning what was relevant in contrast with twisting the facts, Hartzenbusch deemed it necessary to add notes to some of his plays, ranging from instructing the actors to delete several lines on stage, to giving lengthy historical explanations. Some footnotes concern terms which may not be clear to the audience (as a person's mispronouncing words deliberately, or due to ignorance). *Un si y un no* (A Yes and a No) has twenty-six such notes scattered throughout the text. In *El mal apóstol y el buen ladrón* (The Bad Apostle and the Good Thief) there is a list of nine Hebrew words used to designate God, with their corresponding meaning. *La ley de raza* (The Race Law) has fourteen notes on names, customs, and supposedly historical data of the time of the Goth domination of parts of Spain. In *La jura en Santa Gadea* (The Swearing at Saint Gadea) there are thirteen notes about El Cid and the eleventh century.

A very good example of Hartzenbusch's way of writing and reworking is his first performed play. Plays he wrote and revised will be listed first. The last to be named will be one he also reworked, which was performed posthumously.

I   *The First Play*

Floresinda, a tragedy in five acts, in verse, imitated from the French, was published by Repullés (Madrid, 1844), and takes place in the palace at Narbonne, no date given.

Act I. Recaredo loves Floresinda, but it is more important to him that his friend Vitimiro vindicate himself in the eyes of King Wamba, even if Vitimiro marries Floresinda. She, in turn, likes Vitimiro's brother, Leandro, believed dead. Rejected by the girl, who mentions his dead brother, Vitimiro suspects he is alive, and goes to war with Recaredo. In act II, Vitimiro admires Recaredo because the chief of the enemy faction surrendered to him without identifying himself. Of course, it is Leandro. Floresinda takes care of him but they do not reveal their love for each other. She tells Vitimiro she is grateful to him because he saved her, but nothing else, and he swears to kill the man she loves, if there is one. She answers that he will not make her hate him. Recaredo attempts to convince him to reconcile himself with Wamba, and to overcome his feelings. In the third act Leandro complains of the change, betrayal, and pretended concern of Floresinda, sure she is going to marry his brother. She denies it and Leandro believes her, but Vitimiro comes with the news that he is once more Wamba's subject and asks Floresinda to marry him. She refuses for the second time and Vitimiro reacts by saying he despises her enough to marry her off to another, only to kill him at the altar. Finally he suspects Leandro is his rival, and imprisons his brother. Floresinda protests, but Leandro says they should pity Vitimiro; he is a traitor to his king, offends Floresinda, and she hates him. Recaredo arrives with the news that the enemy seeks Leandro and wants the door of the castle open to the king. Vitimiro puts Recaredo in charge of the defense.

Act IV sees Leandro in prison, wishing Floresinda to escape with a servant and look for the king; he will fight his brother but without a conspiracy. Perhaps "Gothic Spain" will free the castle. They take so

long in saying they love each other that Vitimiro appears. Leandro
threatens to kill him but still has to fight against the king. Floresinda
blames herself for bribing the soldiers. Vitimiro agrees she is guilty,
but everybody will live if she marries him. She refuses, and Leandro
urges her not to give in. "Love me so much you wish me dead," he
says, thinking so to triumph over his brother. Vitimiro orders Leandro executed in front of Floresinda, to harm her more. She asks
Recaredo to help her and kill her, too. He assures Vitimiro that
Wamba will pardon him, but Vitimiro prefers to die with his rival. He
doubts Recaredo's friendship, but when the latter agrees to do
whatever his friend wishes, they reconcile. What Vitimiro wants is
revenge against Leandro and Floresinda.

Unsure of Recaredo's loyalty, in act V Vitimiro has elected another
avenger; Recaredo wasn't furious enough. Vitimiro, recalling his
childhood with his little brother, Leandro, feels remorse, but one is
dead already. Frantic because he realizes he has committed a crime,
when Floresinda appears and offers him her hand if he spares
Leandro, Vitimiro says it is too late and blames her. Recaredo is
reprimanded for having obeyed. However, the one killed was the
trusted third party Vitimiro had sent to kill Leandro, and Recaredo
was waiting for his reaction. All embrace and ask forgiveness. As a
result, Vitimiro asks Floresinda and Leandro to marry; he will go back
to his king. But there is a drawback: Floresinda had taken poison
before offering to marry Vitimiro. She dies, and Vitimiro kills
himself.

This tender story of brotherly love and friendship is neurotic and
repetitive, with obscure passages and sudden changes of mood,
feelings, and thoughts. It is not clear how a character can be loyal to a
king and work against him at the same time; Recaredo's self-sacrifice
for his friendship with Vitimiro (portrayed as the epitome of evil)
seems more important than his love for Floresinda. The play bears no
date, but King Wamba was in power from 672 to 680, centuries before
the inhabitants of the Iberian peninsula could be called "Spanish."
This, however, is not what is wrong with the play, if we read the
critics of the time it was written, rewritten, and published. At the end
of the 1844 edition, a note by Hartzenbusch states that this free
translation of the *Adelaida Duguesclin* was made in 1827, with
different characters and title, and retouched in 1830. Deviations from
the original are allegedly due to Voltaire's works being forbidden in
Spain at the time, and to the fact that these were the author's first
dramatic lines in verse.

Eugenio de Ochoa, in his prologue to the Paris edition of Hartzenbusch's selected plays (1849, published in 1850), says of *Floresinda* that it was the author's first translation in verse, but alien to the art he took as his model, *Abufar*, by Ducis, an earlier translation by Dionisio Solís, not well received because it contained two marriages but no deaths. Guided by this, Hartzenbusch translated Voltaire's *Adelaida Duguesclin*, putting in it two deaths: one, that of the bride, to make the marriage impossible. Since Voltaire's plays were forbidden, he further disguised the original by moving the action to Spain, to the times of King Pedro; making it impossible to be recognized by its own author; still not satisfied, he suppressed the confidents, but kept the types and the language of French knights of the fifteenth century as Voltaire wrote them, reflecting the latter's way of thinking and speaking in all his characters, no matter how purportedly Spanish. Later he reworked it, placing it in the seventh century, making even more improper the ideas of an eighteenth-century French philosopher concerning the Gothic reign of Wamba. It was not accepted by the Madrid theaters.

The importance of *Floresinda* in Hartzenbusch's production lies in the fact that his great love for the theater led him to explore, experiment, and practice the art blindly, not only without a guide, but without learning from his trial-and-error method. His reworkings of this particular play followed his whim at the time, adding, changing, and complicating the action, without making it better. A foreign conflict viewed by an eighteenth-century Frenchman, complicated to conform to what the author thought was public taste, retaining concepts and language of the French original, gained nothing when transported to Gothic times.

Other titles listed as translations from Voltaire are: *Nanina, La escocesa (L'Ecossaise,* The Scotchwoman); *El hijo pródigo (L'Enfant prodigue,* The Prodigal Son); *Edipo* (Oedipus); *Doña Leonor de Cabrera (Adelaida Duguesclin)*, which ended up as *Floresinda*, already discussed. Additional translations and imitations from the French, sometimes unidentified further, are: 1823, *El español y la francesa* (The Spaniard and the Frenchwoman); 1829, *El tutor* (The Tutor), from *Le tuteur*, by Dancourt; 1829, *El regreso inesperado* (The Unexpected Return), from *Le retour imprévu*, by J. Fr. Regnard; 1831, *La escuela de los padres* (School for Parents), from *L'école des pères*, by A. Piron; 1839, *Función de boda sin boda* (Marriage without a Wedding), from *Les noces sans marriage*, by Picard; 1842, *El abuelito* (The Grandfather), from *Le bon papa, ou la proposition de mariage*, by Scribe and Mellesville; 1843, *El novio de Buitrago* (The Bridegroom from Buitrago), from *Le voyage interrompu*, by Picard, or so Eugenio Maximino Hartzenbusch speculates; 1846, *El doctor capirote o los curanderos de antaño* (Doctor Dunce or the Healers of Yesteryear), from *Les empiriques d'autrefois*, by Scribe; 1847, *Los dos maridos* (The Two Husbands), from *Les deux maris*, by Eugene Scribe; 1849, *La independencia filial* (Filial Independence), no more details given; 1861, *El padre pródigo* (The Prodigal Father), from *Un père prodigue*, by Alexander Dumas, the younger.

More translations, imitations, and partial adaptations are listed by Hartzenbusch's son, including a number based upon foreign pieces in manuscript form, such as *Merope*, by Alfieri (1854); *Emilia Gallotti*, by Gotoldo Efrain Lessing (1838); *Marion Delorme*, by Victor Hugo, in part only; several works by Molière; and an array of bits and pieces, for which reason the reader is referred to Eugenio Maximino Hartzenbusch's catalogue for more information.

II   *The First Play Performed in a Public Theater*

El amo criado (The Master Servant), a comedy by Francisco de Rojas, reworked in five acts by Hartzenbusch, was published by Yenes, Madrid, 1841, first performed in the Liceo Artístico (Artistic Lyceum) of Madrid, no date given, and then at the Cruz Theater, April 24, 1829. The new version is in five acts, as opposed to two of the original. Nothing has been improved—only more added. Written in the vein of the ever-popular intrigues of Calderón, Lope, and others, a gentleman going to meet a girl betrothed to him by mail sends another man's portrait, since he is not so good-looking. Misunderstandings result, including a maid's suitor leaving the premises via a balcony (placing the reputation of the lady of the house under suspicion), people assuming false names, characters hiding or appearing after a long absence and being mistaken for someone else—but all leads to a happy reunion of the right couples.

This type of puzzle, in expert hands, is delightful when not moralizing per se, but in the fastidious fingers of Hartzenbusch it becomes a maze. Adding what he deems necessary to the plot, he overlooks the fact that while he knows what he wants to do, the audience does not. Eliminating vital information, present in the original play, to replace it with further complications, makes the action impossible to understand and kills audience interest. The same line is followed by Hartzenbusch in his adaptations of Spanish classics, some listed by his son as only partial and in manuscript form, while others were performed. The list includes: *Dar la vida por su dama* (To Give His Life for His Lady), by Coello; *Por su rey y por su dama* (For His King and for His Lady), by Bances Candamo; *Guárdate del agua mansa* (Beware of Still Water), by Pedro Calderón de la Barca; *Los empeños de un acaso* (The Obligations of the Unexpected), by Calderón, about 1829; *La confusión de un jardín* (The Confusion of a Garden), by Agustín Moreto; *El médico de su honra* (The Doctor of His Honor), by Calderón, 1844; *La esclava de su galán* (The Slave of Her Lover), by Lope de Vega, 1847; *Desde Toledo a Madrid* (From Toledo to Madrid), by Tirso de Molina, in cooperation with Bretón de los Herreros, 1847; *Sancho Ortiz de las Roelas*, 1852; *Progne y Filomena*, by Francisco de Rojas Zorrilla, 1854, partial manuscript; *La prudencia en la mujer* (Caution in Woman), by Tirso de Molina, 1858; *El perro del hortelano* (The Gardener's Dog), by Lope de Vega, 1862.

III   Sancho Ortiz de las Roelas, *Hartzenbusch, and Lope de Vega's*
La Estrella de Sevilla

This play being a reworking of an adaptation, it presents a good opportunity to show the way that works of art are treated by critics and scholars, writers and dramatists. Lope de Vega's original text, *La Estrella de Sevilla* (The Star of Seville), has been the object of a long, intricate controversy as to the question of authorship. Somehow this aspect has caught the attention of scholars much more than the powerful drama itself. The inconclusive proofs are that there are two versions of the play, one 3,029 verses long, the other a *suelta* (issued separately) with 2,523. The date of composition or publication of each (often confused and not necessarily contemporary), is uncertain, the *suelta* appearing to be late seventeenth-century, whereas Lope died in 1635. The longer version ends with words by a character named Cardenio, who attributes the play to himself, while the *suelta* ends with similar words in the mouth of Clarindo, who credits Lope de Vega with the authorship. The text used for my analysis is that of the *suelta*, published by Federico Sáinz de Robles (Aguilar, Madrid, 1954), in his *Obras escogidas* (Selected Works) of Lope.

Federico Sáinz de Robles laments, in both angry and humorous terms,[1] the questionable validity of Foulché-Delbosc's opinion that *La Estrella de Sevilla* is not by Lope de Vega, and the fact that many

Spanish scholars have taken his word for it. Sáinz de Robles agrees
that the supposedly poor versification is due to authors and actors,
such as Andrés de Claramonte, who corrected and worsened the
play. Claramonte is the subject of a controversy that becomes an end
in itself, bypassing the contents of the play. However, Sáinz de
Robles praises the reworking by Cándido María Trigueros, calling it
rather a reconstruction, a version presented in England by Lord
Holland in 1817. The reworked play by Trigueros, titled *Sancho
Ortiz de las Roelas*, was performed in the Cruz Theater of Madrid in
1800, when the writer was already dead. The editions of that year, of
1804, and of 1813 sold out. The play was also performed in 1821 (in
1820 the English public bought out the annotated edition of Hackey
J. Smallfield).

The plot of *La Estrella de Sevilla* by Lope is as follows: In act I, in
the alcázar (palace) of Sevilla, where Sancho el Bravo, now ruler of
Castilla, has taken his court, everybody welcomes him and places
themselves at his service, so long as his mandate is not detrimental to
the city. The new king and his trusted Arias comment on the beautiful
women they have seen along their parade through the city, discuss
their identity, and especially one who has captivated King Sancho:
Estrella, sister of Bustos Tabera, a prominent official of the town.
Arias suggests praising Bustos to the king.

Gonzalo and Fernán come to ask for the vacant post of general at
Archidona; the king offers it to Bustos, who happened to arrive but
was not looking for an assignment. The king, taken by the sense of fair
play of the young man, wants him in his palace. Subtly Sancho finds
out Bustos is single, and mentions giving his sister a dowry. So many
honors put Bustos on guard. Estrella and Sancho Ortiz de las Roelas,
accompanied by two servants, discuss their forthcoming wedding.
Bustos tells Sancho, aside, of his visit with the king, and that he wants
to give Estrella a dowry. Sancho says he should have told the king his
sister was already promised to him.

The king, pretending to take a stroll, drops by Bustos's house. The
sovereign should not visit his vassal, the young man says; if he wants
to see Estrella he can do so after she is married, when the house will
be ready to receive such a high visitor. With these words they go to
the palace. Arias remains behind and offers Estrella riches on behalf
of the king, but she pays no attention. Arias then offers a slave her
freedom for admitting the king to Estrella's quarters that night.

In the second act the king enters Estrella's house just as Bustos
arrives, and in the dark draws his sword. The king identifies himself

but Bustos rejects his claim; the real king would not stoop so low. In an aside, however, Bustos tells us he has recognized the intruder. As servants enter, the king flees; the guilty slave confesses to the irate master of the house, who promises to take her to see the king. Arias, informed by King Sancho of the failed attempt, advises that Bustos be killed; the king's whims are law, and since the death cannot be justified, it must be done in secret. He knows just the man for the job, the Andalusian Cid, Sancho Ortiz de las Roelas.

At daybreak the dead body of the slave is seen in the wind. Bustos explains to his sister what happened and that he must leave, but that very day he will have her marry Sancho Ortiz and let him be the guardian of her honor. The king, ready to receive Sancho, has prepared two papers, one with the name of the person to be killed and the other saying it was by order of the king, who adds he is not proud of the deed. Sancho asks why the secrecy if the man is guilty, and requests that if the transgression is not very serious the man should be pardoned. The sovereign implies the crime was against his person, and the offender should be killed by surprise. Sancho says he will not assassinate anybody, and tears the paper telling who gave the order so he will not be apprehended and punished. He asks as a reward only that the woman he elects be given to him in marriage, to which the king agrees.

Clarindo gives Sancho Ortiz a paper from Estrella, announcing the good news of their wedding. Sancho rejoices, but first he has to execute his orders and opens the paper. A soliloquy follows in which he tries to decide what to do in such a dilemma, concluding that he must choose between justice and obedience, and then let God punish the king. Sancho tries to see Bustos, and with a futile excuse provokes his friend, who falls in the fight. Sancho asks him to get up and kill him, but Bustos dies after telling him to take care of Estrella. Sancho then tries to end his own life, but Pedro de Guzmán and Farfán de Ribera prevent him from doing so. Sancho calls himself a Sevillian Cain, but refuses to divulge the reason for the duel. He wants to carry Bustos home in his arms. Meanwhile Estrella is dressing for the wedding; her mirror falls and breaks, a sign of bad luck. When people arrive with the news, she speaks as if delirious.

In the third act the only information given by Sancho is that he had to kill Bustos and did so. The king urges him to confess even if it implicates him, or die. Estrella comes, asking that she be the one to judge Sancho. The king gives her a ring as identification so she can enter the prison at Triana and take charge of the prisoner. He rejoices that it will end that way, but also has the impulse to free Sancho. In jail, Sancho asks musicians to sing because he is going to die. The judges appear and insist that he speak, but he only repeats he killed Bustos, without giving a reason.

Arias arrives with orders from the king to tell the truth; Sancho is ashamed that the king should ask such a thing, since he saw him tear the incriminating paper. Sancho implies he is behaving like a king, and he who obligates himself should keep his word. The accused triumphs over himself by keeping silent, and thus shames the one who is not speaking; each person has to act according to who he is. The town officials say Sancho offends the city with his behavior, leaving Sancho alone with Clarindo. Sancho speaks as if demented, to which the servant answers, commenting upon an allegory in which Sancho, speaking as if he were in the next life, complains about the injustice of the world. Clarindo follows suit, saying they are in hell; honor causes these misfortunes, and laughs at those who keep their word. Estrella, dressed in black and covering her face with a veil, comes asking for the prisoner. She sets him free, but he wants to know who she is. Sancho refuses his freedom; he wants to die for what he has done, and they part.

The king is still puzzled by the silence Sancho keeps, to which Arias says that he is under the obligation to keep the word he gave Sancho Ortiz. King Sancho knows it is unworthy of him to let him die, but he will be left in a very bad light if he confesses. Arias suggests that the city fathers be bribed to pardon the prisoner, who can be made a general somewhere; Arias himself will then bring Estrella, so the king can marry her off to a nobleman. Pedro de Caus brings the news that Sancho went back to his cell after the episode of the lady with the ring, and the king orders Pedro to bring Sancho to him secretly. Then he tries to intervene with the judges, asking exile for Sancho, but their verdict is that he must die.

Estrella arrives, while from another side Sancho is brought in. The king, before the assemblage, again asks Sancho to state the truth, and tells Estrella he has a husband for her. She asks for Sancho to be freed. Farfán objects to the miscarriage of justice. Finally the king confesses, and Sancho elaborates on it. If he accepts exile, the woman he wants for a wife has to be given to him, as promised. Estrella, however, says she cannot bear to see her brother's assassin in bed and at her table. Sancho similarly states that he cannot live with the sister of his best friend, whom he murdered. The lovers go their separate ways as the play ends.

Cándido María Trigueros's *Sancho Ortiz de las Roelas* was very much available as the basis for Hartzenbusch to produce his own version. The *sueltas* of Trigueros's version that I found are dated 1814, printed in Madrid, and 1818, printed in Valencia. In this adaptation, the first words we hear are spoken by the king to Arias, saying he knows his efforts are futile: as long as Bustos Tabera keeps his sister, Estrella is out of reach. The scene of the triumphal entrance of King Sancho into Sevilla and the comments on the city and its beautiful women are not found in this version. A further difference is that the preliminaries and the furtive intrusion of the king into Estrella's house are described, not staged. Estrella told the king, as he recalls, that she was too little for a wife and too much for a mistress, words repeated by Hartzenbusch. When Bustos asks the king permission to give his sister in marriage, the papers have already been drawn.

Following Lope essentially, changing some scenes and possibly giving a lift to the whole play, we find that Trigueros made his characters less explicit in their thoughts, feelings, and actions than in Lope's play. The end is handled somewhat differently also. Estrella doesn't want to live if Sancho is sentenced to die. When the king finally confesses to giving the order for Bustos's death, Guzmán merely comments there must have been a reason, and no further inquiry is made. Estrella, married on paper to Sancho, declines to accept him as a husband, deciding to enter a convent. Sancho releases her from her promise, as does the king; but Sancho will not stay in the monarch's service in Sevilla, choosing to go to Granada to fight the Moors. The scheming Arias is exiled, as the king belatedly recognizes the superior qualities of his subjects.

Trigueros's ending attempts to vindicate the king, somehow ennobling him by virtue of the fact that he realizes what fine people he has around. But, is Sancho really that superior? His loyalty to the king is total because he is the ruler; in his righteousness as a good citizen for whom the king is the supreme power in every way he destroys three lives: Bustos Tabera's by murdering him; his own and Estrella's by ruining their existence forever. The bitterness in Estrella's heart and the pain she must endure make of her the only really superior character. Her brother is killed by his best friend, Estrella's husband-to-be, on their wedding day. She loves Sancho, but how can that love survive even if it was in obedience to the king and in fulfillment of his duties that Sancho killed Bustos? The latter might receive a reward for his innocence in another life, but Estrella has to live with the pain. Sancho's future is ruined also because his blind allegiance to the sovereign, no matter how honorable, has deprived him of his best friend and the woman he loves, whom he must never see again.

Trigueros, despite the suffering and death inflicted on the protagonists, chose these words to end his play:

> King (to Sancho): Go with God, and leave time
> to have your deeds admired,
> for I am surprised
> to see so many in one day.
> Oh passion! Oh bad advice!
> Farfán: That you recognize that is enough.
> Everybody: Heroism begins
> where weakness ends.

The main difference in the handling of the theme by Lope, Trigueros, and Hartzenbusch resides in how each depicted the king. His treachery, fueled by the evil Arias with his bad counseling, his support in plotting to abduct Estrella, and the subsequent intrigue to dispose of Bustos, are developed one step at a time by Lope. Early in the play, there is already doubt in the king's mind about the propriety of his scheming. All his underhanded actions become a burden, when his ally Arias suggests that a king must keep a promise given. This twist could be taken as a further proof of Arias's less-than-noble character; in a way he rejoices on seeing the king in trouble. By suddenly changing his line of reasoning, adding more bad advice on how to deal with those who must judge Sancho Ortiz, he makes the king waver. Trigueros went a step beyond in trying to restore a bit of dignity to the king, owing to his high station, not because he does more than to confess to a crime for which he, as king, is not going to pay. Hartzenbusch, in turn, made no attempt to show the king in any but the worst light, making him appear blunt and ill-tempered. It is difficult to believe that he could feel love or attraction for anyone. Hartzenbusch dispensed with many necessary explanations, especially about Estrella and what happens in her house at different times.

IV Hartzenbusch's Version

La Estrella de Sevilla ó Sancho Ortiz de las Roelas (The Star of Sevilla or Sancho Ortiz de las Roelas), tragic drama of Lope de Vega, reworked by Cándido María Trigueros and arranged in four acts by

Juan Eugenio Hartzenbusch, was published by Cabaut and Cía., Buenos Aires, no date. This version's first performance at the Príncipe Theater, Madrid, took place March 2, 1852. The action is set in Sevilla, in 1285.

Act I opens in the alcázar (palace), where King Sancho "el Bravo" complains to Arias that he loves Estrella, and being "almost divorced," wonders why he can't have her. Arias agrees, noting that the king, after all, is the ruler. It has been impossible to win over her brother, Bustos Tabera, to get to Estrella, to whom he has spoken only once, at which time she said she was too little for a wife and too much for a mistress. King Sancho even resorted to buying off a maid in order to gain entrance to her quarters, but instead he ran into Bustos; the servant paid with her life. Arias encourages the king to punish Bustos, who in turn might kill Estrella. Bustos requests an audience with the king; tired of looking after his sister, he wants permission to give her in marriage, so her husband will watch over her honor, to which the king agrees.

Once alone, the monarch schemes to sentence Bustos to die and to have Sancho Ortiz de las Roelas, whom people call the Cid of Sevilla, execute the order. Sancho asks the king if the man to be killed in secret is guilty, because if so, the sentence should be carried out in public. The king answers yes, he dared draw his sword to the royal person. This is enough for Sancho, but he does not want to assassinate anybody. The king is annoyed by this attitude, especially when Sancho refuses a paper protecting him from prosecution if caught; he asks only to be given no other such cases. Since Sancho is single, the king offers him as a reward the woman he would like to marry, no matter who she may be. With this promise the king gives Sancho a paper with the name of the man he must kill. Shortly after, Clarindo takes to Sancho Ortiz a paper from Estrella with the news that her brother is arranging their marriage. Sancho wants to see Bustos, but first looks at the name on the paper. It is that of Bustos Tabera. The only solution to the resulting dilemma is to die in a duel with him. To provoke it, Sancho tells Bustos he does not want his sister for a wife, and after a heated argument both men go out to fight.

Estrella is dressing for the wedding in act II as Teodora complains that the ceremony is going to be secret. Maybe that way the king will stop annoying her. Clarindo enters, stating in very lyric tones that he delivered the paper to Sancho. Guzmán brings word that Bustos has died of a sword wound inflicted in a duel next to the king's chambers. The body is brought in, and as Estrella laments that Ortiz would not help her brother, she is told Sancho Ortiz is the killer. Her impulse is to kill him; when the young man arrives he is made prisoner. He explains that he and Bustos fought a duel but cannot reveal the reason. Estrella asks why, but Sancho replies only that he killed his best friend justly, without a motive, that it was an atrocity but not a crime.

In act III the king tells the judges that if Sancho Ortiz gives no reason for killing Bustos, he is his enemy. He complains to Arias of such silence and of the advice Arias gave him, which the king had followed. Arias now believes Sancho must be saved, since the king gave him his word; otherwise everybody is going to be against him when the truth is revealed. After debating his course of action, the king decides to see Sancho, who will be exiled. At this point Estrella arrives, accompanied by twenty citizens, who leave when she is granted an audience with the king. She wants to take charge of the prisoner, invoking an old law. The king agrees, asking that she be merciful, and tries to have her listen to him, but she says she will only do so next to her brother's corpse. The king, alone once more, suspects Estrella knows everything, and with a passing reference to the fact that Rome has not recognized his marriage, decides to offer Estrella the crown.

Arias brings Sancho to the presence of the king. The young man maintains his silence; furthermore, he has eaten the paper incriminating the king, despite orders to explain his action. Sancho says only that Bustos lifted his sword against the king. When it occurs to Sancho that perhaps the king had designs on Estrella, he rejects the thought, hoping Bustos will forgive him from heaven. He begins to realize, however, that Estrella is not aware of these things. The girl offers Sancho a horse and freedom, which he declines, refusing to be a fugitive, but still refuses to talk. Estrella tells Sancho that the king has been after her ever since his arrival in Sevilla; Bustos is dead because he stopped the king as he entered her house. She guesses Sancho must have killed Bustos, and will pay for it with his life, so she wants to set him free. Sancho, who did not know the king wanted Estrella for himself, realizes that if he dies or goes away she will enter a convent, equivalent to death in life. If he flees, he loses both his honor and Estrella. Thus, Sancho prefers to die.

In the fourth and final act the king feels remorse for having caused so much harm. He asks the city officials to administer justice to Sancho, not only a gentleman but a dignitary of Sevilla. The king attempts through Guzmán to influence the sentence in favor of the accused, saying that he must have had cause to duel with Bustos. In a similar effort made through Farfán, he suggests that exile be imposed as an alternative to death. Thereby he appears merciful without revealing his guilt. However, the city officials' verdict is that Sancho be beheaded.

Arias advises the king to pardon Sancho, observing that he knows something he is not telling. Sancho is brought in with Estrella also present, and the king urges the accused to confess; he replies torn papers can't say much. Then he is advised to heed the king and Estrella and leave Sevilla. He is pardoned by the king, who overrules the judges' objections. Farfán tells the king Sancho and Estrella were in love. (How he knew is not explained.) The king, in a sudden change of mood, decides to try to save that love, and confesses that he killed Bustos and that Sancho saw the killing and took the blame. The judges leave, since Sancho is free, and nobody is going to prosecute the king. Estrella demands to know if the king's story is true. The king reiterates it, ordering both Sancho and Estrella to leave the city. Sancho wants to tell Estrella everything but she refuses to hear him out, adding that Bustos forgives him in heaven as she forgives him on earth. Hartzenbusch gives no clear indication of what happens next, whether they leave together, marry, or what the solution is.

Absent from this version, also, given the changes made by Hartzenbusch, is the refusal on both parts to marry once Sancho is cleared of the murder. The king has no reason to admire his subjects since his confession makes that development impossible. This version preserves the dramatic impact only a Lope de Vega could impart, but adds the intricacies and twists for which the Romantic playwright was known. The lyricism of Clarindo when he takes the paper from Estrella to Sancho and when he tells her he has accomplished his mission contrasts very sharply with the brusque reactions of the king and his abrupt decisions, such as disposing of Bustos. The men keep silent no matter what their behavior will do to the woman they most care for, Estrella. It is absurd that they would place honor and obedience, duty and similar considerations before the peace of mind of the woman for whom they risk everything. ›She does not seem to matter at all as a person. None of these men thinks for a moment about her side of things. In their own view they risk what is dearest to them, their honor, for her. But by "protecting" her, the men are destroying her life. Hartzenbusch seemingly keeps Estrella in the dark until the third act, when we discover she knew about the king's attempt to enter her room, while Sancho knew nothing. By having the king lie in an effort to ennoble him, the issue is even more confused because Estrella is kept more in the dark, and the author dismisses this point by having her refuse to hear Sancho's version.

V   *The Critics*

Antonio Gil de Zárate, in his evaluation published in Hartzenbusch's selection of Lope's plays in 1853, one year after his own version of *Sancho Ortiz de las Roelas*, says of the *Estrella* that it was a description of the death of Juan Escobedo (1578), secretary of Don Juan de Austria, dealt by Antonio Pérez under the orders of King Felipe II, and written to air the unsavory persecution of the henchman for having obeyed the king. By placing the action in the time of Sancho IV, of whose epoch Gil de Zárate says little is known (as was true of the Tabera and Ortiz families), Lope protected himself. These comments can be found in the 1923 edition, pages xxxi–xxxii. It is interesting to note here that Hartzenbusch, for all that he followed Trigueros, must have been acquainted with Lope's version, and the legends and conjectures surrounding Lope's themes, since Hartzenbusch began a play, *Doña Juana Coello* (of which only a fragment exists), dealing with the Antonio Pérez incident. Whether or not this particular episode was historic—as implied by the existence of Bustos Tabera street in Sevilla and the coincidence of dates with the reign of King Sancho IV—different dramatists placed it in the latter's time, 1284–1285. If Lope did it to recount a dismal episode close to his times, he no doubt cast a shadow on King Sancho, but Lope is justified to some extent by the lack of information on that king, coupled with the possibility that the protagonists were, in real life, those depicted. In contrast, what little exists of *Doña Juana Coello* is tinged by Hartzenbusch's insatiable thirst for complications, as he invents an adulterous relationship between Antonio Pérez and the Princess of Eboli.

Nicholson Adams said of Hartzenbusch's version of *Sancho Ortiz de las Roelas* that it was flavorless and devoid of lyricism, following Trigueros's rather than Lope's original drama. The commentary of Sturgis Leavitt in *La Estrella de Sevilla y Claramonte*, published in 1931 by Harvard University Press, alludes to two incidents that occurred in Lope's time, one involving King Felipe IV, the Count-Duke of Olivares and the Duke of Albuquerque, and the other concerning the mysterious murder of the Count of Villamediana (1622), as possible sources for Lope's play. Leavitt eliminates Calderón as a possible author since his dramatic production is later, an obvious conclusion, and studies the date assigned by Emilio Cotarelo y Mori to the play, 1623, based on a reference to an edict concerning collars and hair length. This allusion is made by Clarindo, a character believed to be interpolated by Andrés de Claramonte, in which case the addition is dated, but not the whole play. On the other hand there are no additional references to Sevilla. Claramonte could have eliminated those extant in the drama already, but did not do so.

Leavitt also mentions plays from other pens in which there is a brother in the middle of things, apparently to criticize Claramonte. If he is the Clarindo of the play, why does he stay onstage as Bustos and Sancho talk, the critic inquires. I see no reference to his staying onstage or leaving; that is the decision of the theatrical director, and the context indicates when a character enters or leaves the stage. Speculation follows as to whether or not Claramonte uses the name Clarindo only in plays appropriated by him, in which case he could have reworked the *Estrella* and added the praises and references to Sevilla. Leavitt insists it is not Lope's work, but it appears that only one person wrote it. Marcelino Menéndez y Pelayo maintained there were interpolations by another hand, probably Claramonte's. Cotarelo y Mori similarly believes that Claramonte reworked it and added the references to Sevilla. To both these opinions, Leavitt replies that those allusions cannot be suppressed and have much of the play left. All these gentlemen might well have been asked if the title doesn't matter at all.

Leavitt looks for similarities between the *Estrella* and several plays by Claramonte. My impression is that Clarindo is not an important character and has little to do with the Cardenio mentioned at the end of the play. One cannot help wondering why the authorship, put in doubt by Foulché-Delbosc (whose word was taken as gospel), seemed the only thing worth studying. Leavitt finds faulty verses as a clear sign of the author's being from the south of Spain, and Claramonte was born in Murcia. He points out a confusion on the part of Lope de Vega of the apples of the Hesperides and the golden fleece, a cultural flaw in someone as learned as Lope. I had the good fortune to attend a conference during which Professor Fred A. de Armas explained his theory concerning this point. His analysis of the so-called confusion, as applied precisely to the *Estrella de Sevilla,* should vindicate Lope for all the controversy this seeming slip has caused.[2]

After citing other scholars on what Claramonte did in various plays and the method followed by some critics, Leavitt concludes that

Claramonte must have written this particular play to be performed in Sevilla, and added the edict on collars and hairdo as a bit of local color when it was to be performed in Madrid. Also, if the Count of Villamediana episode was the inspiring factor, Cardenio is almost an anagram of Clarindo, he says.

This writing by professor Leavitt was anxiously awaited by Henry Thomas in 1930, when he published his second edition of *La Estrella de Sevilla*. Thomas leans on Foulché-Delbosc to affirm that Lope de Vega is not the author; he laments having no Spaniards around who might clear up for him obscure passages, and bemoans that S. Madariaga had to leave the country. This preliminary statement speaks poorly of Mr. Thomas's command of Spanish. Just the same, he claims to have corrected a few things and two notes, but neglects to tell us what they are. He points out that other than an article by Griswold Morley, all critical studies deal with the authorship of the play, conjecturing about the elusive Clarindo (not found to date, and whom Cotarelo y Mori considers fantastic). In light of previous opinions, Thomas changes his "formerly attributed" to Lope to simply "attributed." The rest of the prologue has to do with his having divided the acts into scenes for the benefit of those who read plays little by little, his doubting that Lope is the author although his name appears in the last verses, and the confusion of the apples and the golden fleece. The date of composition is deemed to be between 1625 and 1634, but if *La Niña de Plata* (The Silver Girl, 1617) is indeed inspired in the *Estrella*, no specific date can be established. Thomas observes anachronisms in the buildings mentioned, existing in the author's times (not in those of the play), and the houses of Bustos Tabera and Sancho Ortiz. After an allusion to the work's *gongorismo* (obscure, conceptual, and difficult style), vocabulary and notes close the book.

Thomas returned to the theme in 1950, making a translation, *The Star of Seville*, published by Oxford University Press, British edition. Condescendingly, Thomas says the play "has long passed as perhaps the best of Spain's greatest dramatist," then proceeds ro criticize the plain verse in contrast with the gongorism he finds. It seems to Thomas that the shorter version of the two known editions is for performing purposes. He believes the theme to be possibly historic, very old, and notes the English reader must take into consideration the honor code of the epoch, accepting certain things, as foreigners do when reading Shakespeare. The action is placed in 1284, the year the real King Sancho became ruler of Castilla and then moved to

Sevilla. Whatever faults Thomas finds in the *Estrella*, he must have found it fascinating since he translated it into English, and mentions that translations into French, German, Italian, and Polish have spread its fame.

Comparing Hartzenbusch's reworking of this classic with its predecessors, Lope's versification is adequate to the scene at hand, without excessive lyric or learned overtones, and certainly contains no obscure and ornate passages and metaphors, as claimed by Henry Thomas. Clarindo is only a servant, not a main character, and in the prison scene, when Sancho unleashes his rage caused by his deception with the morality of the world, complaining that rectitude has led him where he is, Clarindo merely agrees with his master, a logical action on his part. Some critics make much of the "delirium scene," when we know very well Sancho Ortiz is not insane, but only besieged by his troubles.

Trigueros's version subtracted considerably from Lope's play, condensing many scenes and long passages performed in the original version. The one who inserts endless florid words into the mouth of Clarindo is Hartzenbusch, perhaps in an effort to conform with those who stated *La Estrella de Sevilla* was full of such speech. Juan Luis Alborg praises Trigueros, who, in the prologue of his *Sancho Ortiz de las Roelas*, expresses great admiration for Lope, and states his intention to rework *La Estrella de Sevilla*, adjusting it to the rules. Believing the first part is long enough to constitute a whole play he reduced most of that to narrative, later developing a few scenes more fully. The good reception of the play encouraged him to try his hand again with another play by Lope. In turn, Hartzenbusch and Bretón de los Herreros imitated the model set by Trigueros and reworked many plays of the Spanish Golden Age, thus being responsible for a renaissance of the national drama.

In my opinion, the word used for such reworkings, *refundición*, meaning literally "melting and recasting," suggests reducing metals to a liquid state. In the melting, it is understood that impurities, extraneous matter, and useless particles will disappear; therefore something will be lost in the purifying process. To make a *refundición* of a three-act play and come up with a new one in four or five hardly fits the word. If in the recasting the essence is not kept, but obscured by additions, the play thus reworked should have been left intact. *Refundición*, as used in the dramatic sense, was meant to update a play so it would be better understood by a particular generation, given changing contemporary attitudes, values, and environment.

The difference between what Trigueros did and what Hartzenbusch endeavored to do is mainly that the former tried to shed
excessive preliminary material to concentrate on the principal action;
the weeding out was followed by a complete cleanup, not harming the
original play but making it more manageable. Hartzenbusch, by
contrast, adds and deletes selectively, but also drops vital material,
adding foreign matter for no reason. He appears not to realize that
while he knows the story the audience does not, and will be discon-
certed by a gap or an obscure passage left without explanation.

VI   *Adaptations of Foreign Themes*

Ernesto, a drama in five acts, in prose, a free translation of
Alexander Dumas's *Angela* (published by Piñuela, Madrid, 1837),
takes place in Cotterets, in the Pyrenees. Ernesto, born rich, lost his
fortune at his father's death and decided to climb the social ladder
at the expense of women who like him.

Primero yo (I Come First), a drama in four acts, in verse (published
by Repullés, Madrid, 1842), was first performed in the Príncipe
Theater, Madrid, April 14, 1842. It takes place in the Escorial,
beginning October 11, 1757. The story revolves around Luciano, a
highly respected man, who married Rosalía for the sake of conveni-
ence, but doesn't love her. Seeking the favors of his niece, Mariana,
he implies that his wife has poisoned him. After she is accused,
Luciano proposes to facilitate her escape if she gives him a divorce.
He pretends to know nothing about a phantom (himself) that has been
frightening Mariana. Rosalía is sentenced to die when she confesses
falsely (her life was ruined). When Luciano, dying because he took
the poison himself, asks Isidoro, an innocent bystander who loves
Mariana, to take his wife to England, he says no, just give her back
her honor. Rosalía will spend the rest of her days in a convent,
praying for Luciano, not seeing anyone, especially not Isidoro or
Mariana.

According to Hartzenbusch, this play is taken from a German
novel, *Alamontade der Galeerensklave,* by Enrique Zschokke, and is
reminiscent of the character of Lady Macbeth, imitated by French-
men of different epochs. Hartzenbusch adds that he started the play
in Bayonne in 1841, and that it did not receive the favor of the
audience because it was not understood.

The title does full justice to the main character: he comes first, no
matter what. Hartzenbusch deemed it necessay to use a Spanish

setting, so he chose the Escorial. Not satisfied with this, he made the king Luciano's accomplice in trying to rid him of his wife, this being by means alien to the Spanish traditions. Isidoro could have explained things to Rosalía much earlier, avoiding trouble and misunderstandings, but then the play would have been shorter. The two women are the only characters that emerge untarnished. Still, the decision by Rosalía to retire from the world to pray for that jewel of a husband rings rather false.

La abadía de Penmarch (Penmarch's Abbey) is a drama in three acts, in prose, translated from the French melodrama *L'abbaye de Penmarch*, by Tournemine and Thackeray (published by Marcos Bueno, Madrid, 1844), first performed in the Príncipe Theater, July 22, 1844. It takes place in Douarnenez, on the coast of Brittany. This play, translated with the cooperation of Nemesio Fernández Cuesta, is an intricate tale of crime, smuggling, treason, rancor, revenge, and immorality. Hardly good fare for a Spanish audience, some expressions and plays on words are totally Spanish.

VII *Magic Plays*

La redoma encantada (The Enchanted Phial), a comedy of magic in four acts, in prose and verse (published by Yenes, Madrid, 1839), was first performed at the Príncipe Theater, Madrid, October 26, 1839. The action is situated in and near Madrid.

A girl is married to an old man under the threat of having her true love sent to the galleys. Magic and the aid of the remains of the reputed sorcerer Enrique de Villena, kept in a phial, help the young woman become a widow. People taking someone else's appearance and incarnations of several kinds achieve the goal; the time in history is suggested with the use of landmarks and names such as those of the king and other people. Although the date when the action takes place is not stated, Enrique de Villena uses old Castillian when he appears.

A warning to the reader, never to the theatergoer, precedes the play. Hartzenbusch apologizes for undertaking such a task as writing a piece about magic and admits to having taken main scenes from three different plays, and perhaps from others he hasn't read. After stating that he didn't like that kind of play, he mentions one of the first he saw, with the complaint that if it had been announced with the proper title he would have known it was that type of theater (the variation is so small one wonders why he didn't make the association).

There follows a short list of printing errors, but the note from the printer is a real protest as to the way the author handed in his material. As in other instances this piece was retouched by the author many years later, in 1862.

Los polvos de la madre Celestina (The Powders of Mother Celestina) is a comedy of magic in three acts, adapted from the French *Les pilules du Diable* (The Devil's Pills), by Ferdinand Laloue and Anicet Bourgeois et Laurent (published by Yenes, Madrid, 1840), first performed in the Príncipe Theater, Madrid, January 11, 1841. It begins in Madrid, ending near Huesca, at the close of the seventeenth century. It is a tale filled with inanities, magic tricks, forced humor, allusions to historic and fictional figures, and probably impossible to perform. All leads to a marriage opposed by a brother-in-law, another suitor, and a witch. This play was also revised in 1855.

Las Batuecas is a comedy of magic in seven parts, in verse and prose (published by Repullés, Madrid, 1843), and staged for the first time in the Príncipe Theater, Madrid, October 25, 1843, taking place in Batuecas, 1488. On the last page the author says he was inspired by two French plays to compose his own: *Thimon le misantrope* (Thimon the Man-hater) by Delisle and *La Volière de Frère Philippe* (The Aviary of Brother Philip) by Scribe, Mellesville, and Delestre-Poirson.

The promising beginning is soon marred by too many things going on without cohesion. Fantasy, magic, giants, dwarfs, transformations, and special effects probably impossible to bring about onstage dilute the testing of people and their reactions to given situations.

Some names are allegorical, such as Fortunio (from riches), Sofronio (science), and Virtelio (virtue); Paulino was a donkey before, and behaves accordingly; other Spanish names are Mari Castaña and don Turuleque. The hazy moral that goodness brings happiness is lost in a maze of good behavior, rewarded in some and punished or ignored in others; a girl marries a prince who turns out to be her brother, while her blind brother is the real prince; the donkey turned man is in charge of the supposed prince, who is told women are birds, and many more things equally confusing.

VIII   *Weak Characters*

La visionaria (The Visionary Woman), a comedy in three acts, in prose (published by Repullés, Madrid, 1840), occurs in Palma de Mallorca. Críspula believes Vicente is after her daughter, but he only wants to buy her house. Another mixup with money, lost and counterfeit, a secret passage, misunderstandings of people's intentions, are added to plain statements made in one act and denied in another—too many explanations of the kind of "as you know" and "yes, and I told you then. . . ." A conveniently dead uncle whose inheritance reaches the weakest character, people who keep quiet when they should speak—all confirm Críspula in her idea, until Vicente turns out to be married. But that is all right, since her daughter's dull suitor is the heir, anyway.

La coja y el encogido (The Lame Woman and the Bashful Man), a prose comedy in three acts (published by Yenes, Madrid, 1843), was first performed at the Cruz Theater, Madrid, June 16, 1843), takes place in Madrid, no date given, and is taken from two plays, one French and one English, with attempted humor restricted to the meek Fabián, so cowardly he is afraid to even get his name straight, and a maid by the name of Tomasa. The story is woven around assumed names, mistaken identities, and fake physical defects to test people's greediness and moral character. It was published again in 1850, with variations.

Un sí y un no (A Yes and a No), a prose comedy in three acts, was published by Rivadeneyra, Madrid, 1854 (performed for the first time in the Príncipe Theater, Madrid, February 18, 1854). The action takes place in Madrid in 1853. An inheritance about to fall in the wrong hands, lost documents, misunderstandings, information passed on from conveniently converging sources, a young man more interested in money than in the woman he purports to love, all lead to the righteous older man marrying a "destitute orphan" who is the real heiress. Introducing a peasant type, Hartzenbusch has deemed it necessary to explain the mispronouncing of words uttered; such vocabulary is footnoted on each page as it occurs. Twenty-six in number, these notes help only a curious reader, since onstage only the words written in the scene are reproduced.

Juan de las Viñas (a prose comedy in two acts), was published by the author in the print shop at the Plazuela de San Miguel in Madrid, 1844, and performed for the first time in the Cruz Theater, March 12, 1844. The outskirts of Madrid at the beginning of the eighteenth century are the scene for the story of a poor soul, Juan de las Viñas, who decides to do everything in reverse since nothing seems to turn out right for him. The attempted humor fails because it feeds on a meek person, and leans on plays on words and silly situations that are not convincing.

IX   Plays in Cooperation with Other Writers

¡Es un bandido! ó juzgar por las apariencias (He Is a Bandit! or To Judge from Appearances), a comedy in three acts, in prose and verse, written in cooperation with D. Manuel Diana and published by Yenes, Madrid, 1843, was first performed in the Cruz Theater, Madrid, May 20, 1843. The scene occurs in Madrid, no date; this play deals with the misunderstandings caused by a betrothal arranged by parents between two young people in childhood who don't know each other.

Jugar por tabla (To Play by the Board, not a meaningful translation of a gambler's term) is a comedy in three acts, in verse, written with Luis Valladares y Garriga and Cayetano Rosell, taken from the French *Gabriela*, by Emil Augier and published by Omaña, Madrid, 1850, staged for the first time in the Príncipe Theater, Madrid, December 18, 1850. It is set in Villaviciosa de Odón, no date. According to Hartzenbusch's son, his father arranged the first act, did not touch the second, and had some part in the third. Fernando and Sofia's marriage is dull and in trouble. Impossible as it is to know what parts were written by which author (despite Eugenio Maximino's note), feelings do not go as far as in other of Hartzenbusch's plays, and dignity is maintained. The harsh words uttered by some of the characters, especially the men, point to our author's hand, but being a play written by three people, after a foreign piece, the whole is diluted to the point that this can barely be considered Hartzenbusch's work.

X   Writing for a Child Actress

La archiduquesita (The Little Archduchess) is a prose comedy in three acts (published by Rodríguez, Madrid, 1854), performed for the first time in the Príncipe Theater on November 8, 1854. It takes place in Vienna, in December of 1646. The plot stems from an historic theme, but Hartzenbusch has developed his own intrigues. It was written, according to the author, for the child actress Rafaela Tirado, who was twelve years old at the time. A promising artist, she died at the age of eighteen.

Mariana de Austria, a child, upon the death of her promised husband, prince Baltasar Carlos of Spain, son of Philip IV, her uncle, is promised in marriage to the king of Spain by her father, Ferdinand III of Austria, who in turn has lost his wife. Leopold, his brother, a bishop, advises Ferdinand to keep the laws of royalty and to marry his niece, who is fourteen years old (he is thirty-eight); Philip IV of Spain is forty-one, and Mariana doesn't particularly want to marry a man that age. Matilde, her teacher, will have to convince her. The latter wears a nun's habit—she promised to wear it for a year while the little archduchess was sick, but the whimsical child liked it, so she keeps wearing it (and confusing everybody). Matilde has two suitors who have not uttered a word to her: the emperor and Per-Afán, who is also her uncle, unbeknownst to her. He is a courtier, preceptor, and thirty-two.

The convincing of the bratty princess is not handled straightforwardly: a jewel is presented to Matilde by the emperor, who doesn't reveal it is from him, and she is confused by that and by an anonymous letter from Per-Afán. Claus, an intriguer, spies on everybody for gain, and the very serious matter of kings marrying, the better to govern, is reduced to a charade. Challenge, posed by little Mariana and seconded by the adults, results in a mock wedding that is made to stick, with each uncle marrying his niece, with the proposed moral that nobody should ask another to make a sacrifice he is not willing to make himself.

Historically speaking, there is little truth in this play; Hartzenbusch admired the child actress, and must have been inspired by the shameless Portuguese in Tirso de Molina's *Averígüelo Vargas* (Let Vargas Find It Out). The death of Prince Baltasar Carlos and the later marriage of Philip IV to Mariana is factual, but the intrigue is strictly Hartzenbusch's. The only character that holds his own is the dignified bishop, Archduke Leopold, whose judgment and counsel are proper at all times. Otherwise everybody speaks the same, whether Spanish, Austrian, young, old, king, or servant. The child expresses herself as an old woman, wise in arts not every woman lives long enough to know or hear about. The actress may have been outstanding, but this role is less than appropriate for such a tender age.

Derechos póstumos (Posthumous Rights), is a *loa* (short laudatory piece), in prose, written to celebrate the anniversary of the birth of Pedro Calderón de la Barca (publisher unidentified), performed at the Príncipe Theater, Madrid, November 8, 1854. Written in prose, instead of the short lyric recitation of years past (usually in praise of the author of the play about to be performed or a member of the royal family), this *loa* seems more like a play. It was evidently written for Rafaela Tirado, since she portrays the precocious Rosita, who knows all of Apolinar's troubles and business. There are several notes by the author: one about the first verse of the *loa* being taken from a play, with variations; the pieces that compose the program; what a *loa* was like in old times; and how much it rained in the winter of 1856 (apropos of description of early theaters, in the open). One more note concerns another performance of this particular piece, and another, fifty lines of very fine print, explains what the author's rights are, including the posthumous.

Vida por honra (Life for One's Honor) is a prose drama in three acts (published by González, Madrid, 1858) and staged for the first time in the Príncipe Theater, Madrid, October 9, 1858. It takes place in Madrid in 1622.

This is another play full of intrigues, unexplained things, and extraneous matter. The count of Villamediana (who in reality died under mysterious circumstances) is depicted as undesirable, given to women, cunning, a gossip bent on destroying reputations, and bringing all sorts of disaster to other people. In the maze of wrong-doings, the king and queen, noblemen, ladies, government officials, and people of all walks of life wander, going nowhere. A secret order in the third act remains secret. Jusepa, depicted as a very young girl, almost a child, follows the pattern of at least two other such characters, Mariana in the *Archiduquesita* (The Little Archduchess) and Rosita of *Derechos póstumos* (Posthumous Rights). She expresses herself in as coarse a manner as the others. Her young years do not justify this lack of vocabulary coupled with concepts and opinions, implications, and conclusions far more advanced than her age.

The historic setting and a few names in no way make this array of misdeeds and miscarriage of justice acceptable even as a fantasy, since it is too closely related by the author to real places and names.

In the second act there is a footnote to the effect that the romance of the count of Villamediana is used with variations, but there is no specific reference to the original or where can it be found.

XI   *Plays with Gothic Themes*

After *Floresinda,* already treated in this chapter, Hartzenbusch picked up the Gothic theme in a different way, not adapting a foreign work. This time it was *La madre de Pelayo* (Pelayo's Mother), a verse drama in three acts, (published by Repullés, Madrid, 1846). It was performed for the first time in the Príncipe Theater on March 24, 1846. The action is in Tui (*sic*), March or April of the year 702. Act one opens as Geroncio, a Roman priest, asks for clemency for his son,

Alicio, a rebel.[3] Vitiza will let him see the young man, and also Luz, who pleads for clemency for the rebels, asks for freedom for Alicio (we are not told why she is interested) and that no taxes be levied; finally she asks for permission to enter a convent, where her daughter, Hermesinda, is already.

Vitiza agrees to everything except the last item; he wants Luz to be his wife, since Goths and "Spaniards" have been free to marry for more than fifty years,[4] but she observes that she married Favila against everybody, her marriage was declared invalid, and her baby boy, Pelayo, taken away from her and abandoned, like Moses, in the Tagus River. By chance the ark in which he was set afloat has come to her hands, but without news of her son, who must be sixteen years old by now. Only if she finds him, and her husband's assassin, will she consider Vitiza's proposal.

Alicio, out of prison, tells Luz that Geroncio took him to Tui, and while the latter was looking for lodging the boy (Alicio) wandered to a dark place where he heard sounds of a fight; a man attacked him, Alicio threw his venabule, killed the man, and fled. Later it was discovered the dead man was Favila. Alicio was made prisoner, along with others, by Vitiza.

In act II Luz doubts the goodness of Vitiza. Alicio, in confession to the priest, discovers he is an adopted Jew. Alicio is, naturally, Pelayo, but since Vitiza does not know it, he has exiled him to Africa as a slave. Luz tries to stop this, but Vitiza objects, insisting they be married, since she found Pelayo and her husband's assassin in one person. Luz reveals to the boy that she is his mother, and he says he did not kill anybody. Vitiza admits he killed Favila, but gives Luz an alternative: either she marries him or he kills Pelayo. In act III, Luz asks Vitiza not to exile Pelayo. Merván, a merchant, brings the news that Pelayo has escaped from the ship that was taking him to Africa and is coming to the palace to kill Vitiza, disguised in his mother's dress. The palace is closed in the belief that Pelayo has had no time to get in, but he has, and sees Luz. She wants to plead with the king, but he has given orders not to let her into his chambers, since he knows about the disguise Pelayo will use. Azael, the Jew who found Pelayo in Lisbon and gave him to the priest, offers his vestments to the young man, but Merván wounds Luz mortally, thinking it is Pelayo in her dress, and she, dying, tells Vitiza that Rodrigo will have his throne and Pelayo will be the savior of Spain.

History says that Luz married Vitiza, who had her husband, Favila, murdered, in order to save the life of her son, Pelayo, the first hero to stop the Moorish invasion in the north of what is now Spain. His tomb, in the rugged mountains of Asturias, in Covadonga, impresses the visitor as few places do. Don Rodrigo, his cousin, was the last Gothic king. Why Hartzenbusch chose to murder Luz in such an inglorious manner is a question that has no answer. There are those who judge her death in this dramatic work as a sacrifice, when actually she is an accidental victim.

The anachronisms committed here are simply that, not poetic license; Hartzenbusch juggles laws and kings to give what he must have thought was dramatic impact to his tale. If King Chindasvinto repealed the law that forbade Goths and natives of the country invaded to marry, it should not be ascribed to his son Recesvinto to have done so. If Favila and Recesvinto were brothers, it makes no sense that Favila's marriage to Luz, whatever her origin, would be fought in such a way as Hartzenbusch describes. This play, dated 1846, precedes *La ley de raza* (The Race Law), dated 1852, and even though it was revised in 1858 the contradictory statements and inaccuracies were not corrected. The fact that Hartzenbusch mentions Alfieri's *Merope* as part of his inspiration adds nothing of value.

La ley de raza (The Race Law) is a verse drama in three acts (published by González in Madrid, 1852); it was first performed in the Drama Theater, Madrid, April 24, 1852. The play takes place in Toledo in the year 653. At the beginning of act I, Gundemaro, a Goth, tells Fulgencio, a Roman citizen and a doctor, that since his sister died after he treated her, by law his life is at the mercy of the dead person's family; if they decide to sell him as a slave, he will buy Fulgencio and use his knowledge to prepare poison for whomever it suits him to eliminate. Heriberta, presumed daughter of the dead princess and about to marry the new king, Recesvinto, gives the doctor a key so he can escape and take a letter to Recesvinto, in which she tells him she is not the daughter of the dead Berengarda, as she had declared to count Bertinaldo and his daughter Gosvinda. The princess had a baby who died due to carelessness, and was replaced by Heriberta; she is really from a city near the Duero River, perhaps Numancia, and not being a Goth cannot marry Recesvinto, since it is forbidden by law. Fulgencio is from Numancia, where after an absence he found his wife and baby girl buried.

Gosvinda is happy about the discovery because she loves Recesvinto; she will see that Heriberta becomes a nun. But Bertinaldo and Duke Egilan plan to kill Heriberta so Recesvinto will not find out about her origin and try to abolish the law. They count on Fulgencio to prepare a poison, telling him it is for another prisoner. He agrees, if they will exile him to Numancia. He writes on a parchment with a venom that kills upon breathing it, but tells Heriberta because he doesn't trust the others. Egilan is elected to take the letter to Heriberta and she asks him to read it to her; she pretends to read it and faints; then she fakes being mad, claims she is a princess, and continues the masquerade in front of Recesvinto when he comes.

In act II we find that Heriberta speaks her mind to Gosvinda and Bertinaldo while feigning madness, and that she has burned all her papers except for a testament (the poisoned document) which she keeps with letters from Recesvinto. Recesvinto tells Egilan it would be wise to put "Spanish" men in command; after all, they have imposed on the Goths their language and religion; they rise while the Goths go down, so all must unite. Egilan takes the opportunity to tell Recesvinto that Heriberta is a "worthless Spaniard". Meanwhile, Gundemaro takes Heriberta a letter from Fulgencio, who has found out his daughter is alive, and wants her to help him locate her. Heriberta pretends before Recesvinto that Berengarda predicted many things, and in order to save himself he should marry Gosvinda; the king is dying and so he orders, she says, adding that she, Heriberta, should be exiled to the Balearic Islands.

In act III the king is dead. If the doctor responsible for his death is not found, many "Spaniards" will be killed. Fulgencio intercedes with Gosvinda, who has not yet married Recesvinto because he is away at war. She states the king died trying to escape Heriberta. Bertinaldo wonders how she got back from the Balearic Islands, but since she is insane she must not be prosecuted. When they round up twenty Spaniards the rest will be pardoned. Now Gosvinda is jealous, having read letters from Heriberta to Recesvinto, and would like to read his to her. Heriberta enters, declaring she was never insane, didn't go to Palma, wants to save her people, and pleaded with the king to tell her about her true origin. He indicated a box, the one containing Recesvinto's letters; the will with the thick poisoned letters was there too, and she lost it in a crowd. Gosvinda says she will exile Heriberta to Africa. Heriberta will pray for her, and if she doesn't make Recesvinto happy she will curse her. Gundemaro finds the box, takes it to Gosvinda, and the noble Heriberta keeps quiet about the poison. In addition she predicts Spain will discover lands far away, beyond the sea.

Gosvinda has died after reading the contents of the box. Heriberta is, naturally, the long-lost daughter of Fulgencio. Fulgencio tries to save Heriberta but she wants to die for her people as a Numantine. Egilan declares Heriberta innocent and the count is accused. Finally Recesvinto shows up; he was being taken prisoner to Froya, but the noble Spaniards saved him. They are all so good that Egilan abolishes the race law as they acclaim Heriberta as queen, so one must presume she is going to marry Recesvinto and free her people.

The innumerable holes and contradictions in this play surpass all other historic liberties taken by Hartzenbusch, such as being very liberal with the word "Spaniard" roughly eight centuries before such a name could be used properly. There is also the question of Gundemaro buying Fulgencio as a slave if he is sold by the family of the dead princess, his own sister. Who is to decide, if he, apparently, is her only family? If she was the mother of a child replaced by Heriberta, there could be no racial difference of any sort. What power could Gosvinda possibly have to send Heriberta or anyone else to the convent? Heriberta's madness makes no sense at all in front of Recesvinto, and we are not told who the rebel count is or what he has done.

The Goths were always reputed to be Christians, so they could hardly convert to a religion they already practiced. How Fulgencio finds out after so many years of absence that his daughter lives is also unexplained. Who the mysterious woman is who aids the Goths against the Basques is not elucidated. We are not told how long the king (called Chindasvinto in most references, but Quindasvinto in this play) was dying. Whether or not he ordered his son to marry whomever Heriberta says, the prince makes no move to verify that. If the king died of poisoning *and* of natural causes, it is difficult to understand why the doctor, who is not Jewish and is not Fulgencio, is being sought after, or why "Spaniards" will be sacrificed.

How Gosvinda came upon letters for and from someone else is not explained, as well as why the generous Heriberta keeps silent about the poisoned will, knowing Gosvinda is going to inhale its fumes; Gosvinda may be a rival, but not a threat, and she did not plot the poisonous document. Why Fulgencio wants a Moorish invasion and for what reason Heriberta predicts the discovery of the New World, are too farfetched.

Hartzenbusch added fourteen notes to his play, the first dealing with the name of the princess whom he calls Heriberta, because the real name of Reciberga was not pleasing to him. There is a question whether the improvement was so great; this man elsewhere names his Spanish characters Tiburcia, Críspula, and Turuleque. In the same note Hartzenbusch casts doubt on whose wife Heriberta became, whether of Recesvinto or his father Chindasvinto, while in note two he places the wedding in the year 653, that of Chindasvinto's death, lacking evidence to the contrary. Hartzenbusch states that Froya's rebellion took place not several years after Recesvinto became king, but before his father died. There was a disturbance then, and our author naturally supposes that it was the rebellion in question, and historians are wrong.

Other notes deal with Gothic laws and how Hartzenbusch arrived at *Q*uindasvinto instead of the normal *Ch*indasvinto, and customs or habits of the times. The remaining notes name no less than four plays from which the author claims to have taken an idea, a verse, a scene. In the third act, scene XIV, there is a note to the effect that for performance eleven verses should be deleted. These explanations are unavailable to the audience and mean little to the average reader. At the very end there is a copy of a document relating to rights and property of plays. It bears no date but mentions 1849 in reference to previous rules and regulations.

XII *Historic Themes*

The term historic, used loosely by more than one author, in the case of Hartzenbusch may be an episode or simply a background, with no real characters portrayed onstage, but with enough references either in the setting or the names used to make the work appear believable. At times, however, there is no clue as to what is historic about a given play, despite its being so classed.

Las hijas de Gracián Ramírez o la restauración de Madrid (Gracián Ramírez's Daughters or the Restoration of Madrid), an historic prose drama in four acts, was first performed at the Cruz Theater in Madrid on February 8, 1831. According to Aureliano Fernández Guerra,[5] and Antonio Ferrer del Río,[6] to mention only two of the critics, it was so badly received by the audience that it was never published. According to different sources, the manuscript is kept in the Municipal Archives of Madrid. A résumé of the plot, together with references to the historic legend are found in the Master of Arts thesis of Pamela Alexander Gill.[7]

The action is set in the year 720, with the title promising a version of a legend treated by other authors before Hartzenbusch (including Fermín de Laviano in the eighteenth century), whose texts Hartzenbusch started to rework, changing them considerably.

The original legend tells that Gracián Ramírez, a gentleman who lived during the Moorish invasion, retired with his family to a castle in Rivas, near the Jarama River. One day, visiting the sanctuary of Our Lady of Atocha, he noticed that the image was missing. He set out to look for it, promising to build a temple in her honor on the place where he found it, a promise subsequently kept. The Moors, believing the construction to be a fortress, tried to stop it, and in Gracián's absence killed his wife and two daughters, cutting their throats. After making the Moors retreat as far as Madrid, Gracián went to thank Our Lady of Atocha, and found his wife and daughters praying, with only scars on their necks. Hartzenbusch, however, dispensed with the miracle, without which there remains nothing extraordinary other than the oft-repeated feat of fighting the Moors. Having done away with the essence of the legend, the playwright added the intrigue of captivity, proposed forced marriages, rejection, and finding a long-lost daughter. The result is not what is suggested by the title, which at least should reflect an important part of the play.

Doña Mencía, a verse drama in three acts was first published (Repullés, Madrid) in 1838, and in 1850, with variations. It was premiered at the Príncipe Theater, November 8, 1838. The action takes place in Madrid at the beginning of the seventeenth century. In act I, Gutierre and Mencía learn through a servant that Inés and Gonzalo are in love. Mencía always wanted to become a nun, and Gutierre, their tutor, was opposed; now she is legally able to enter a convent without his consent, but she shouldn't force Inés, her sixteen-year-old sister, to do the same. A double shadow covers her birth: she was illegitimate, and her mother, a Mexican heretic by the name of Beatriz, was executed by order of the Inquisition.

Mencía implies to Inés that Gonzalo also is a heretic, and the young girl writes a letter renouncing his love to save him. She adds, however, that she hopes Mencía will suffer as much as she does. When Gonzalo, who is forty years old, arrives, Mencía likes him for herself. In act II Mencía shows Gutierre a paper from Guillén Herrera, the real father of Inés (Alfonso de Lanuza, who is Mencía's father, was until then presumed to be Inés's, too). It is not known why Leonor, Mencía's mother, did not reveal what she knew.

Gonzalo comes to tell Mencía he is leaving; someone has denounced him to the Inquisition. She speaks to him in rather strong and amorous terms, offering to help him in his plight. He has a portrait of Luther, speaks against the Inquisition, and she reacts. Inés and her maid witness part of the scene and learn that Gonzalo had a love affair in Lima, that the lady went to Mexico, and, of course, he is no other than Guillén, Inés's father. Gonzalo hides in the house. Gutierre tells Inés he wants the heretic that has entered the house; because Mencía robbed her of his love, Inés asks that they not marry if Gonzalo is saved, to which Gutierre agrees because he loves Mencía. As tutor or guardian, he will see that Gonzalo and Inés marry if he gets Mencía. Gutierre heads the party apprehending Gonzalo. Inés reveals to Mencía she knows about her love and hopes they suffer, since both of them have made her so unhappy. However, she requests clemency, and then Mencía shows her the letter.

Act III opens in the convent; Inés is ready to profess. Mencía confesses to Gutierre that she lied when the inquisitors questioned her; she has been married to Gonzalo, who is likewise in a convent. The sisters beg each other's forgiveness, each saying she was worse than the other. Inés now does not want to become a nun. Meanwhile Gonzalo has escaped and comes to ask Mencía to go away with him, and, since she knows his daughter, to take her along. Only then it is revealed that it is Inés. But suddenly it develops that Gonzalo had an affair not with Beatriz, the Lutheran, but with Leonor, the virtuous mother of Mencía (and supposedly Inés), a Peruvian, married in México. His daughter is twenty-six (and if he is forty . . .) When Inés arrives, having professed already, these complications are explained to her. The inquisitors apprehend Gonzalo, who will be imprisoned for life, and Mencía, realizing she has married her own father, takes his dagger and kills herself. Inés, meanwhile, had fainted.

This intricate plot, devised as if with no preconceived plan, leaves a number of things unexplained, produces many sudden changes of mood and thought, and, instead of showing how difficult life was under the Inquisition, succeeds only in airing the cruelty of a woman, Mencía. The unhappy lot of the innocent Inés contrasts with the amorality of the rest of the family. The use of Peruvians and Mexicans of the seventeenth century, who are also made heretic, is baffling. How could people born in the New World, of Spanish blood, be Lutheran and go to Spain to live?

Alfonso el Casto (King Alphonse the Chaste), a verse drama in three acts (published by Repullés, Madrid, 1841), was performed for the first time in the Cruz Theater on June 25, 1841. Set in the year

792, it begins in a valley of Galicia and ends in Oviedo. Alfonso, dethroned by his brother Bermudo, hides in the house of his nurse, not far from a monastery in a valley of Galicia. Sancho, Count of Saldaña, heads a search party after having joined the forces of Ordoño, his future brother-in-law. Jimena, Alfonso's sister, is also missing. To atone for the guilt of their father, Alfonso had vowed that Jimena would never marry but live in his house as a nun, to which she agreed. She is now posing as the nurse's daughter. Sancho gives her a note. When Alfonso tries to leave for the monastery, Jimena reads the letter, learning of Sancho's desire to help Alfonso. When the search party returns, Ordoño informs Sancho that he has been elected king and so must appear a traitor in the eyes of the real king, Alfonso. The Count of Saldaña, disgusted by the maneuver, refuses to marry Floresinda, Ordoño's sister, and the two men fight.

Act II occurs in Oviedo. Alfonso orders construction of a passage between the palace and the church of the Savior, as well as a coffer, a pew, and other items for his sister. The Count of Saldaña is reported dead; Floresinda is now to marry someone else, and her brother, Ordoño, loves Jimena. But Sancho Saldaña recovered and fled to Oviedo, fainting near the church where Neftalí, a Jew, found him; Bernarda, the nurse, who cares for him but reported him dead, refuses to show Silo the corpse. Sancho vows to stab Ordoño with a dagger, piercing an incriminating paper that Jimena has. She shows it to Ordoño. Silo tells Alfonso what he knows without revealing the name of the count; the king does not want to know, but instructs Silo to give the man a sword and money and order him to go away.

Complications increase when Ordoño sees a man hiding in the church. Sancho appears with the unconscious Jimena; she fainted upon recognizing him. He had been observing her in the garden for over a year, when a woman who saw him threatened to tell the king. To avert the harm he promised to marry Floresinda. Jimena says she does not love Ordoño, promising to turn over the letter to her brother. She plans to become a nun, and thinks Sancho should leave Oviedo. Sancho had found Jimena fainted next to the chapel; she thinks he was going to rape her, but it must have been Ordoño. Alfonso is puzzled to see Jimena and the count together, and has Sancho taken prisoner. Jimena has lost the paper that she showed to Ordoño earlier; who can have taken it? Her pleas that Sancho is her husband are to no avail, and the count is sent to a dungeon.

In act III Bernarda's nephews are pardoned, and Ordoño's sentence is reduced; he protests that he loves Jimena, but Alfonso replies that for that he is exiled, and, for the same offense, the Count of Saldaña is sentenced to die. Ordoño argues the king never loved, to which he agrees. Jimena intercedes on behalf of the count without success and quarrels with her brother, affirming that her vows are no longer valid and that she will marry Sancho. Alfonso threatens to kill him one minute later, but offers to spare the count's life on the condition that she reject him; he then threatens to marry her to Ordoño. Further complication ensues when Bernarda says Jimena is her daughter, not Alfonso's blood sister, though she nursed both of them. The king reacts by confessing that he has loved Jimena for the past fifteen years. Of course, this was a trap set by Bernarda to make Alfonso reveal his incestuous love of which Ordoño had told the nurse.

It is falsely reported that the count has been executed, but the victim is actually Ordoño. Jimena arrived in time to save him with the pardon she stole. Alfonso orders Jimena and Sancho to leave, marry, and never see him again. The people will be told that the count was blinded and jailed and that she has been sent to a monastery.

This brief summary only suggests many holes in the story, the inconsistencies and confusion created by the lack of reasons on the part of the characters to act the way they do. Hartzenbusch continues to drop names, changing spelling to suit his taste, and calling the population "Spanish" in the eighth century. Without quoting all the versions found in encyclopedias and history books, let us give a summary of what they say: King Alfonso el Casto (the Chaste), so called because he did not have marital relations with his wife, reigned in Asturias from the year 791. Reputedly a model king, very kind to his subjects, but relentless against his enemies, his mandate seems to have been clouded by the behavior of his sister Jimena, of whose clandestine marriage to Sancho, count of Saldaña, was born Bernardo del Carpio in 794. For an act of treason not clearly stated in history, the count was blinded and sentenced to life imprisonment, and Jimena sent to a convent.

Hartzenbusch includes an appendix at the end of his play in which he tries to clarify what crimes may have been punished so cruelly in Gothic times. Disobedience by a girl who married against her parents' wishes (or her brother's if he were her guardian) usually only brought disinheritance, at the discretion of the relatives in question. Treason or conspiracy against the king, however, was punishable by death, and such a sentence, if commuted, could be changed to blindness and life imprisonment. Hartzenbusch quotes several historians, and is aware of what history says, but feels free to make alterations, since it all has the quality of a fable. Thus, he has added the character of Ordoño, modeled after one he found in the *Primera parte del conde de Saldaña* (First part of the Count of Saldaña), by Alvaro Cubillo de Aragón, from which he admits imitating somewhat the first two acts.

Hartzenbusch, in his zeal to correct or improve upon history, wanted to erase the note of cruelty from the reign of Alfonso el Casto, and to give freedom to the unfortunate count of Saldaña. This aim, however commendable, only makes things worse when, instead of making the count a traitor to justify the sentence, he imputes to the king (who earned the term *chaste*) an incestuous love. The appendix is of little use to an audience that cannot even be aware there is one.

XIII *Mistaken Identity*

El bachiller Mendarias o los tres huérfanos (Learned Mendarias or The Three Orphans), a drama in four acts and in verse, was written in honor of the actress Matilde Díez. Published by Yenes (Madrid, 1842), it was performed at the Príncipe Theater in the same year, then published again in 1850, with some variations. Set in Soria in the year 1388, it deals with the identification of Juan as son of Pedro el Cruel (Peter the Cruel) of Castilla. The task is complicated by Hartzenbusch; the historical king had eight illegitimate children by at least two women, called "ladies" from Castilla, and this son is by another virtuous woman from Sevilla. The author produces two documents (not substantiated by history) to cover up the intrigue. Explanatory material, if known, is withheld by the dramatist.

Guilt and innocence are so confused that even the author seems to have trouble unscrambling the true Mendarias. The real bastard, the legitimate son of the man who raised him, and the female bait, Elvira, become hazy to him, and more so to the reader. The notes to the play are irritating, explaining that Elvira, in her ignorance, mispronounces words, not in keeping with her status (the "virtuous" lady from Sevilla, mother of one of the king's illegitimate children, raised her as a daughter). With minimal historical substantiation, Hartzenbusch devised a play using historic background and figures, but overlooked what some of the characters suffered because of their ancestor's faults. Don Juan is thrown in jail and forgotten (he is one of the two crucial Juans of the story). There is an intermediary with both false and genuine documents, a servant, not as loyal as one might expect. For no reason, Mendarias will be pardoned if he becomes a priest, but imprisoned if he chooses marriage; he decides on the latter.

Honoria, a verse drama in five acts and two parts was published by Repullés (Madrid, 1842) and performed for the first time at the Príncipe Theater, Madrid, May 6, 1843, as well as in 1850, with variations. It takes place in Sepúlveda, Segovia, in 1468. Desideria and Honoria were entrusted to Inés by a peasant woman who raised them. On her way to pray for the sick Inés, Honoria meets Jimén; they fall in love, but he says they must keep it a secret for three years, refusing to tell her who he is or to find out anything about her. Time elapses without a message in the tree where he occasionally left her one. Desideria resents the fact that Bonifaz, rejected by her, turns to Honoria. Jimén appears; his uncle having died, he asks Inés for Honoria's hand. The uncle had asked him to locate his long-lost daughter and make her his heiress. It is suspected that Honoria is his cousin and Desideria the child of a renegade Moorish woman. Desideria, on the sly, looks at two medallions believed lost, but Bonifaz finds them. It seems that Honoria is indeed the countess.

In act II, all move to the count's mansion in Segovia. Bonifaz, accused of treason, brings word that the queen frowns upon Jimén and Honoria sharing a house. Desideria knows that the dying count wrote his daughter a letter asking her to enter a convent if his wife were unfaithful. In act III Honoria writes Jimén that they must live separately; after a long scene reiterating their love, which will persist at a distance, they part. Desideria is envious. Later Honoria maintains that her father ordered her to leave the world and that Desideria and Jimén should marry, to which he objects, ending Part One.

At the beginning of the second part, however, in act IV Desideria and Jimén are married. At a hunt with Garcillán and other ladies and gentlemen Desideria is wounded by a stray arrow. Honoria, now a nurse at a convent with Dr. Almoravid, is very ill and leaving Segovia. Desideria is said to be unhappy, envious, and resentful that Honoria forced her to marry Jimén. The latter plans to suck the poison from the arrow (shot by Bonifaz) and perhaps die, but Honoria has done it already. In act V Honoria, seemingly near death, proclaims she is not a Christian. Jimén goes alone to the cemetery, finding three masked men and Honoria, who recovers. Taking Jimén for a priest, she confesses that the doctor gave her a brew so that while apparently dead, she could be taken out of the convent. With the doctor's arrival, it is revealed that Desideria is the true countess and Honoria the illegitimate child of a Moorish woman. Thus, Desideria will enter the convent; Honoria and Jimén refuse to marry.

Among many obscure points is the question of why Desideria should abide by the orders of a man who was not her father, and pay for the guilt of her mother. She is innocent, except for having switched the medallions in childhood. Honoria could have straightened things out at the convent before she entered, or attempted to learn the truth so concealed by the several hands that disposed of her and Desideria. Notes found at the end include an acknowledgement that Hartzenbusch copied the end in part from a Moreto play, but the reference lacks clarity; that in the fifth act there is a bit of *Romeo and Juliet*; that changing medallions is a common thing without resorting to any French source, and that he reworked this play after deciding that *El bachiller Mendarias* should not be performed.

XIV   El Cid as Protagonist

La jura en Santa Gadea (The Swearing at Saint Gadea) is a verse drama in three acts, published (Imprenta Nacional, Madrid) in 1844, corrected by the author in 1867. The first performance was in the Príncipe Theater, Madrid, May 29, 1845. The action develops in Burgos and its surroundings in the year 1073. In act I, Queen Alberta, widow of King Sancho II, treacherously assassinated by Bellido Dolfos in the siege of Zamora, prepares to return to her native Germany (she has no children and cannot succeed her husband to the throne). She wants to favor the Cid in some way; he says he only has two friends, the queen and his cousin Alvar Fáñez, having fallen into the king's disfavor by opposing an unjust war. The chief decides, not the soldier, so the Cid remained loyal to Sancho, but was unable to save him from the assassin. Alberta knows Alfonso won't reign in Castile until Bellido is punished; the queen counts on the Cid for justice, and to make the new king swear that he had no part in the killing of his brother. If Alfonso resents this, the Cid will go elsewhere. Alberta advises him to marry first, and he confesses his love, nursed for seven years, for a young lady whose name he does not know, though two metal hearts in a hermitage represent their love.

Alvar Fáñez reports that Alfonso has gone to Galicia with troops, suggesting Alberta marry the Cid and be queen. . . .[8] They refuse. All leave except the Cid; Jimena and her maid arrive; they reveal their names and swear to marry. Gonzalo Ansúrez, enamored of

Jimena, tries to make trouble, insinuating that if Sancho exiled the Cid, and Bellido, accused by him, is missing, something is suspicious. Courtiers announce that García, brother to Sancho and Alfonso, has lost his mind and Alfonso now reigns in Galicia. Alberta insists on the oath that Alfonso was not a traitor to his brother. He refuses, saying twenty thousand soldiers are witnesses. The Cid suggests that if he is innocent, there is no need for the show of force, and the king agrees reluctantly to the ceremony. He plans that afterwards Jimena and Gonzalo will marry, but learning of Jimena's love for the Cid, he agrees to retract his word to Gonzalo and offers his sister Elvira to him. The Cid complains that nobody seems to want the oath except him. The king argues that if people see him swear they will think he is a criminal, so he will take the oath in private. Gonzalo brings news that he has killed Bellido. Alvar Fáñez, who, to further complicate the intrigue, also loves Jimena, threatens to kill Gonzalo if he does not leave her alone. With all present, the Cid asks the king to swear. Gonzalo says Bellido confessed but added he did it to serve the Cid, who then accuses Gonzalo of jealousy and challenges him to a duel, which the queen tries to stop.

In act III, the king and Gonzalo go to Saint Gadea, and the latter tries to predispose Alfonso against the Cid. The king's chair has fallen, which Alfonso perceives as a bad omen. If he goes through with the ceremony and the Cid wins the duel, Alfonso decides that Jimena will enter a convent. That fate also awaits Alberta upon return to her country, but the playwright further tangles the loves by revealing that she loves the Cid, and tells Jimena.

The Cid awakes from a sleep in the chapel and tells his dream of conquering the Moors. Before the duel, which supposedly Alberta had forbidden, he pardons Gonzalo. Jimena gives him the metal heart and watches the duel from afar, receiving false tidings that Gonzalo has won. Then Alvar Fáñez comes, saying he fought with the weapons of the Cid in his place, and won. This time the Cid fights and wins, and Gonzalo confesses that he lied before; he further reveals to Alfonso that the latter's sister Urraca ordered the assassination of Sancho, which he carried out, thinking to please the heir-apparent. The king swears, but the bell does not ring until he swears for the third time. Alfonso then exiles the Cid for a year; he, not to be outdone, says not one, but four years. Jimena remains in the palace instead of becoming a nun, and Queen Alberta goes home to enter a convent.

Among liberties taken by Hartzenbusch both with history and the

Cid epic is the weighty role given Queen Alberta, a doubtful if not imaginary person. It is falsely asserted that the Cid killed Ramiro, king of Aragón, when that death remains a mystery, and there is no reason the Cid should be involved. Jimena and the Cid were not only already married when he was exiled, but had produced a son, dead in childhood, and two daughters. All this and much more was known to Hartzenbusch, as he indicates himself, appending to the 1844 text some thirteen notes, ranging from the name of the queen (whose homeland was unknown) to challenging the age of the Cid. As with other Hartzenbusch plays, several revisions were made of this one, one of which was published in 1867.

XV   *A Religious Play*

El mal apóstol y el buen ladrón (The Bad Apostle and the Good Thief , a verse drama in five acts, is an imitation of the old Spanish theater. Published by Casas y Díaz in Madrid, 1860, it was performed for the first time in the Circo Theater in Madrid, February 25, 1860. The setting is biblical, a valley near Ephrem at the time of Christ. In the first act Dimas, once accused by Nacor of thievery, endeavors to kill him, having previously slain the latter's wife and children. Sara saved Nacor and his daughter Betsabé, entrusting the girl to Dimas with the fiction that she is a sister he did not know he had so he will take care of her. Betsabé calls Dimas Jesaí at his request, because he is sought after for his many crimes, and wants the girl to remain ignorant of his reputation. As she is baptized, Judas and Dimas ask for guidance, and she foretells their fate.

In act II, the Jews denounce Jesus because he expelled them from the temple as they were conducting their business. Nacor offers Pilate to make up their losses, and asks for a maiden as an adopted daughter. Betsabé is brought in; having learned who Jesaí really is, she wants to retire to a cavern to pray for him. She knows also by divine revelation that Dimas will die crucified. Pilate denies her petition, declaring his love for her. Procla, Pilate's wife, first scolds, then repudiates, him, because she follows Christ.[9] Pilate says of Judas that he killed his father in order to marry his mother. Judas reports that Dimas will surrender if his sister is left with the mother of Jesus, informing Procla that Betsabé is the daughter of Nacor, unbeknownst to Dimas, who loves her but thinks she is his sister. Procla decides to give Nacor his own daughter, but Dimas attacks him, wounding him mortally, with a subsequent revelation of identities. As Procla summons the soldiers, Judas helps Dimas escape.

In act III Judas is apprehended for undisclosed reasons, and Anás tells Judas to identify Jesus with a kiss, since he looks so much like his cousin Yago. Dimas wants to take Betsabé (now called María) away; she answers that she only loves him as a brother, exhorting him to follow Jesus. Dimas recalls that once he saved the Holy Family, not knowing who they were, and the Child, who must have been a month or two old, spoke to him.[10] Now, he wishes he could bring Nacor back to life. María believes his repentance. Pilate makes advances to María, but an angel touches her, covering her with leprosy, and Pilate ceases to want her.

In act IV, María's leprosy extends to the doctor and soldiers present, while she is cured. Procla relates to Pilate a dream (with a portion of the Credo) in which he is responsible for the death of Jesus and asks that He be released. In a further complication of motives, Judas visits Dimas to try to save his soul, but suddenly tries to stab him. Longinos brings the news that Pilate has freed Barabbas and that Jesus is to be crucified. Dimas is prevented from attacking Judas and taken away to be crucified also.

The last act opens as Barabbas takes María to a cave, where Dimas alleges he had concealed his inheritance, part of which belonged to Barabbas's father and part to María's. She recites a Lord's prayer of sorts as Judas appears, fleeing from Golgotha. María invokes the goodness of Dimas as a brother and how he saved the Holy Family; the cross of Dimas and a supposed representation of salvation are seen. Anás, who also knows about the buried treasure, arrives. A poisonous gas emanates from the floor of the cavern, reaching to a person's knees; if breathed it is fatal. This was to be the vengeance of Dimas, disposing of Barabbas and María and preventing her marrying Pilate (which she hadn't considered). Following the gratuitous arrival of Procla, there is an earthquake, and a vision by María who relates that a thief is saved and an apostle damned, and Judas is led away by demons.

Five plays are cited as sources used in part by Hartzenbusch. He also lists nine Hebrew names given to God, with their translation, and in act V adds another, this time in Chaldean. At the end of the play there is a license for performance dated November 1859, and another giving permission for the drama to be printed, dated December of the same year. Hartzenbusch allegedly concocted this play as a challenge to prove he could do a dramatic presentation of the passion of Christ without showing any member of the Holy Family, as was decreed during a time when many prohibitions were enforced at the whim of the restored king, Fernando VII, labeled "el deseado" (the hoped for), subsequent to the Napoleonic invasion. Whatever the reasons for such a measure, Hartzenbusch did decide to write a play on the subject; reception was varied. Antonio Ferrer del Río criticized the absence of Christ in a play about Him, despite being precisely the one who authorized its performance, while Aureliano Fernández Guerra estimated that it was the work of a genius such as Hartzenbusch's to create a drama in which the main characters are never onstage. There are also those, such as Brett, who compare this play to the *autos sacramentales* of Calderón. What is harder to defend are the gaps in the story. The title suggests a play suitable for performance during Holy Week and Easter, but rather than actually treating the Passion, this is a fantasy on the life of Dimas; the implied main theme is treated as very secondary, restrictions on showing the Holy Persons notwithstanding. Even worse, it contains no moral teachings; Dimas has done little to achieve salvation, unless God sees only certain things and ignores others.

Aside from the logical notion that the protagonist should be onstage, and by association it has to be Christ, the story really revolves around the bad apostle and the good thief, only they are not as good and as bad as one might expect. The treason of Judas, unforgivable, is not atoned for by his repentance; Hartzenbusch makes him even worse than history. But he goes overboard to save Dimas, whose story the play really is, though he is not vindicated in any way except by the words of Betsabé, which sound more ignorant and credulous than good. Judas's betrayal of the Son of God, and the circumstantial belief in Him of a thief crucified at the same time, did not suffice for Hartzenbusch, who makes Dimas so unscrupulous, so undesirable a member of society, that his being saved seems a sacrilege.

Judas's treason must have seemed insufficient to merit his damnation, so Hartzenbusch has him attack the man whose soul he went to save, while Pilate adds the information that Judas killed his father so he could marry his mother.

It is hard to accept that Dimas may be saved when there is not a word about his victims. Why Betsabé prays for him and tries to save him is also incomprehensible. He killed her family, including her father, in front of her eyes, and would have killed her if he had known her true identity. A life of crime and thievery is rewarded by salvation at the cross, from where he murders those in the cave. Even if Hartzenbusch acknowledges taking portions of different plays, the mixture so produced leaves one with enormous doubts about divine justice. Why be good and abide by the commandments if that only brings punishment, while a dissolute life leads to salvation?

XVI *The Posthumous Play*

Heliodora o el amor enamorado (Heliodora or Love in Love) is a *zarzuela* (musical play) in three acts, written in prose and verse (Gullon, Madrid, 1880). It was performed for the first time in the Apolo Theater, Madrid, September 28, 1880, and is set in Crete, no date. A note before the title informs the reader that an earlier version of the same play was printed in 1864 under a different title, as a mythological musical comedy of sorts. To ease the problems of staging, it was reworked and given the present title. No dates are given and it is unclear when Emilio Arrieta composed the music. At the end of the play a note states that it is considered a posthumous work, performed in honor of the author, who had died in August of the same year.

The action revolves around worship to Heliodora, who restored the dignity of the family (under Venus nobody could be sure who his father was). Cupid also wants to love, but Venus complains that he wants to make her a grandmother. She fights Heliodora with her arts and influence with the gods. After an intrigue with transformations and various tests, Heliodora and Cupid are reunited in heaven before the altar of Hymen. The intricacies of the plot go in many directions at the same time, making it necessary to simplify the résumé. It remains a mystery why the oil in the lamp of death, which Venus obtained from Pluto and gave to Telefron, is spilled by Heliodora on Cupid. To cure him, she has to marry a horrible Negro. Heliodora will die if she does not marry Aristeo, but if she dies, Cupid and Crete will be saved—from what is never clear. Not too convincingly, Cupid and Heliodora end up with butterfly wings.

CHAPTER 3

Hartzenbusch and Los Amantes de Teruel

I The First Version by Hartzenbusch

THE splash made by the dramatic version of *Los Amantes de Teruel* (The Lovers of Teruel) merits a study, no matter how superficial, of the ripples raised in all directions. The negative aspect of its success is that many scholars deem this account as the only one worth anything. Some label it the definitive version of the legend, but evidently have made no effort to research earlier versions, from which Hartzenbusch took what he wanted. A drama in five acts, in prose and verse (Cuesta, Madrid, 1879, third edition), it was first performed in the Príncipe Theater, Madrid, January 19, 1837. The first act takes place in Valencia, the rest in Teruel and its environs, in the year 1217.

The play opens in the palace of the Moorish king of Valencia, revealing a very ornate bedroom with desk, two small side doors, a big one in the center, and a window with lattice and draperies. A man is lying on the bed. Zulima has asked the jailer, Adel, to take to the harem a drugged captive she used to see from her garden, loaded with chains. Adel, reluctant to do so, fears the amir will find out when he returns and punish him. Zulima, who believes the captive to be high born, wants to know what was written with blood on a cloth they found on him, along with a jewel. While Zulima searches, a spy, Zeangir, comes out of hiding to say he has heard everything. He looks where she was rummaging, discovers the cloth on the bed, and reads it. When Adel inquires as to what it says, Zeangir doesn't answer.

Adel doubts the captive is a prince, despite his strength: he broke the chains and tried to scale the walls of the dungeons, but did not attempt to buy his freedom with money. Zeangir leaves without a word, and Zulima enters with smelling salts to revive Ramiro, asking

Adel to find someone who can read the cloth. The captive revives, startled by the light, and tries to conceal the cloth. Zulima tells him she is Zoraida, daughter of Merván, who rules the palace in the absence of the king of Valencia. She offers Ramiro his freedom, but he says Merván took his possessions when he fell prisoner. She asks his identity and learns that he is Diego Marsilla, from Teruel. Diego has loved Isabel since childhood but, being poor, her father gave him six years to make money to become acceptable as his daughter's husband; otherwise she would marry a rich suitor. Diego goes to war, and returning to Teruel, falls captive as the time limit is about to expire.

Zulima, who liked him immediately for herself, argues that Christian women have hearts of snow, and since their men usually have a wife and another woman on the side, she will be the other. When he refuses, Zulima is angered, threatening to bring Isabel as a slave, because Zulima is the sultan's wife, not Merván's daughter. Diego gives her the cloth, adding that he has heard her husband is coming and that Merván is a traitor who is going to massacre those in the palace that night. That is the message written on a rag he found, using a brush made from his hair, and dipped in his own blood. Adel announces the return of the king and hides Diego, while Zulima produces a poisoned dagger. Zeangir orders that Merván be executed and that a coffin be sunk, not specifying where, with somebody (unnamed) inside. The second act begins in the house of Pedro Segura, in Teruel. Mari-Gómez, a servant who speaks in Latin from time to time, announces the arrival of don Martín to her master don Pedro, who has just returned from an undisclosed location. He bids the visitor enter, as he never hides from an enemy; Martín presumably wants to proceed with a duel postponed because of Pedro's absence from Teruel. Martín enters, naming Domingo Celada without giving further details, Pedro recalls the offense, Martín now reveals that during his illness, he discovered that Pedro's wife took care of him, and therefore he can't raise his sword against him; he offers to let Pedro take his life. With such a virtuous wife Pedro doesn't want to risk dying, so the duel is suspended. (Here there are so many contradictions that it is difficult to understand Pedro's behavior and words.)

Pedro inquires as to Martín's son Diego and the likelihood he will return on time, alluding to a promise he wouldn't want to break. The gentlemen exchange swords and Martín leaves. Pedro's wife, Margarita, enters, to discover that Martín knows who she was and that she has saved her husband's life. He praises her while she kisses first his feet and then his hand. Isabel announces a servant of Rodrigo de Azagra who wants to speak to Pedro. When the women are alone, Margarita tries to persuade Isabel to marry Azagra, as he is a good catch. Besides, she should obey her father, because that is the way all girls marry, including herself. Isabel complains; suddenly her mother talks to her in more affectionate terms and reveals that she has been doing penance; she wears a hair shirt and offers her life for the well-being of her daughter; she decides she will break the promise made to Azagra.

As Rodrigo and Margarita talk, he learns that Isabel has given away all his gifts, which means she still thinks of Diego. Rodrigo plans to fight with him. Margarita wants her husband to choose, but Rodrigo alludes to certain letters he found on the body of a Templar who became a monk in order to atone for having raped a religious woman. The monk, whose name was Roger de Lizama, accused himself of adultery and died in the line of duty. Rodrigo found the letters when burying Lizama; as all were signed by Margarita, he kept them. "They are mine, I am the adultress," confesses Margarita. The blackmailing Rodrigo offers the letters in exchange for Isabel. Pedro will receive them if Margarita fails to persuade her daughter.

In the third act Mari-Gómez admits Zulima, disguised as an Aragonese gentleman, to the Segura house. She drinks water instead of wine, eats nothing, and succeeds in seeing Isabel, whose parents are not home. Zulima pretends to come from the Holy Land and Isabel asks if she knew Diego; yes, she says, he came back to Spain, was imprisoned in Valencia but is now free. The Moorish queen liked him and eventually he gave in to her love in exchange for his freedom; the king returned, punished both of them, and Diego is dead. Isabel faints as Margarita arrives, while Zulima, leaving the jewel taken from Diego, exits. When Isabel recovers she calls Diego an ingrate, and the queen an adultress. Mari-Gómez ventures the thought that maybe the young man was lying. Isabel insists she will not marry Azagra, as Margarita begs her to heed her father and her mother's pleas. Desperately, Margarita reveals she was an adultress after becoming a mother, and has been doing penance; in her oratory there are hair shirts and dried blood. Azagra, who has the incriminating letters, will show them to her father unless Isabel will marry him. Of course, Margarita isn't asking her daugher for any sacrifices. Although Margarita thinks she is not being fair to her daughter, she believes she is saving her husband's honor.

The fourth act is in two parts. In the first, Mari-Gómez helps a reluctant Isabel dress for the wedding; her mother has gone to take care of Jaime, the judge's son, and may be late for the ceremony. Rodrigo arrives, having read Marcilla's letters; he states that he will be satisfied to be Isabel's husband in name only; they can live separately, either in the same house or Isabel in Teruel and he in the court of Aragón. She will be free to do what she pleases, suggesting that includes even refusing to marry him. As a gesture of good will Azagra returns all the letters—except one.

When Don Pedro comes, Rodrigo calls off the wedding. The father scolds Isabel, arguing that he owes him very much, with the result that she agrees to marry Azagra. Pedro says the time allotted Diego is up, and at the signal the ceremony will take place. They all leave except Martín, who is alone when Margarita comes looking for her husband. She asks him to run to the church with the news that Diego is alive; Margarita takes time to tell Martín how Diego sent Jaime Celada ahead; Diego saved the life of the king and is free, but Jaime was wounded on the way to Teruel. Rather than sacrifice Isabel's happiness, Margarita decides to undergo the shame of having her guilt made public.

The second part of act IV opens in the outskirts of Teruel, where Diego and Adel are seen tied to a tree, with a few thieves around them. The vespers bells sound as the men are robbed. Diego asks one of the thieves to show some of the jewels in Pedro Segura's house. The robbers laugh and are about to kill Diego when a stray arrow routs them. A young man—Zulima in disguise—appears and explains that the amir sentenced her to die, and since Diego saved her life she repays him in turn. She wounded the messenger and reports that Isabel is already married, because Zulima had told her Diego was dead. Diego reaches his father's house to learn Celada recovered and talked, but that Martín arrived at the church too late. Diego, enraged, wants to kill Isabel and Rodrigo. Meanwhile Adel finds Zulima and kills her as the king had decreed.

In act V, Isabel, married now as her mother once wished, faces a contrite Margarita. Isabel is left alone in her room in Rodrigo's house as Diego enters through a window. She first says it is unwise for him to be there, and that she married willingly, then admits a secret forced her to do so. When Diego denies surrendering to the queen of Valencia, Isabel begs his forgiveness and says she loves him, but asks him to go away; the honor of Azagra is in her hands. Diego wants to kiss her forehead but she refuses. He discloses his duel with Rodrigo, who was badly hurt, and has threatened revenge on everybody, and Pedro is on his way to see him. Isabel, suspecting Rodrigo refers to the letter he still possesses, wants to go to him before it is too late. She tells Diego she loathes him, asks why he came back, since he has doomed her, and Diego falls dead. Isabel's parents arrive, verify that the young man has expired, and Isabel falls, embracing Diego.

The foregoing summary will suffice to show what an intricate tale this is. Among things that need explaining in the 1836 version are: How could the queen see a prisoner from her garden if he was in a dungeon? By what means did Diego break the chains and why did he waste time pulling out his hair to make a brush to write on a cloth, in the dark? Couldn't he have used a finger? How could Diego tell time in the darkness of his prison? What does Zulima intend to do with the dagger produced in the first act? Why is Pedro glad he won't die, being that Martín doesn't want to fight but will let Pedro take his life? Margarita credits herself with saving her husband's life, but on what basis is not clear. She is suddenly ready to favor a daughter she has ignored for many years, and shows too much concern for her husband's honor for it not to sound like fear for herself.

Rodrigo has a key to Isabel's room and has been spying. Who let him do all that? He suddenly changes from blackmailer to altruist, willing to be husband in name only, a switch in behavior that needs explaining, as he has always been aware of Isabel's love for Diego. The letters Rodrigo gives Isabel are not identified properly, but since he made separate reference to her own, we must guess these are Margarita's. Why does the mother go home with the news that Diego is alive, and not to the church, where she knows everyone is? Diego, announced in the house, enters through a window, conveniently without iron grill. These are only a few of the absurdities and loose ends.

This play's first performance was, according to contemporary chronicles, a smashing success. Mariano José de Larra, then a drama critic at the top of his fame, reviewed this Romantic effort in his usual exalted manner. As a result of certain criticisms and opinions expressed in different ways (in addition to the playwright's habit of rewriting everything), *Los Amantes de Teruel* was retouched and reworked until in 1849 the version that is most widely known was published. A detailed examination of the latter will reveal changes, suggestive of the author's aesthetics and working habits.

II *The 1849 Version*

The stage is the same as for the first edition, with lamps, large flower vases, incense burners, and other ornaments. As before, there is a man lying on the bed, drugged, with a cloth next to him, and the Moorish queen of Valencia and her servant Adel talking directly above him. Zulima wants to flee with Adel and the captive on the bed, whom they call Ramiro. Her husband the amir has gone to bring another woman to share his bed despite promising his wife not to do so. Zulima has a poisoned dagger ready to kill the king or use on the captive if he rejects her. He does not revive, and as they wonder what is written on the cloth, Zulima leaves to find smelling salts. Osmin comes out of hiding, reads the lettering and leaves, telling Adel only that he should alert the king. Adel speculates upon how Ramiro wrote anything in the dark, or how he broke chains and doors. With Zulima's return, the captive revives, screaming at the light. Zulima identifies herself as Zoraida, caring for him by order of the queen, Zulima, who loves him and spared his life.

The young man unfolds the story of his love, revealing that he is Diego Marsilla and that the time limit is about to expire. Zulima says it is in her power to return him to prison, bring him the news of Isabel's wedding or even better, bring her as a slave, and then she reveals her true identity. Diego says that in the absence of the king the queen should know, so he gives her the cloth, saying that Merván is about to attack the palace. She asks how Diego is so well informed, to which he replies that he overheard the plot, broke the chains, made a brush of his hair, dipped it in his own blood, and wrote the message, so it would be conveyed via the food basket. He fell asleep and woke up in that room. He offers, if given a sword, to defend the king. Osmin returns and joins with Diego and Adel to fight against Merván's Moors.

Act II opens in Pedro Segura's house in Teruel. Pedro explains to his daughter Isabel that he has just returned from Monzón, where he went with Rodrigo de Azagra to defend the young king. Pedro owes his life to Rodrigo, who saved him from Roger de Lizama, a madman, sick with remorse, who attacked Pedro in his lodging. As a reward Pedro promised Rodrigo Isabel's hand, without consulting her. He realizes that was unwise; if only Roger had killed him!

Isabel marvels that her father is not afraid to die, but dares not break a word of honor given in such a manner. Teresa, the maid, announces a visitor, whom Pedro reluctantly agrees to see, sending Isabel out of the room. As in the 1836 version Martín Marsilla mentions Domingo Celada without any reason and refers to the duel provoked by his calling Pedro a miser, but postponed because of Pedro's absence and Martín's illness. The duel is off, as a masked person, who turned out to be Margarita, cared for him, so he won't spill her husband's blood. The conversation turns to Diego, who must return within the stipulated time or Isabel will marry Rodrigo de Azagra.

Margarita tries to convince Isabel that Rodrigo is a better prospect than Diego, arguing that she has to obey her father, as Margarita did her own. When Isabel protests, her mother becomes confidential; she has been doing penance for fifteen years, and would give her life for the happiness of her daughter, (although she hasn't shown her much affection). Isabel is puzzled, especially by her mother's revelation that she has been wearing a hair shirt. Teresa announces the arrival of Rodrigo, and Isabel hides to listen. When Rodrigo perceives that Margarita is on her daughter's side, he states he has certain letters he found on Roger de Lizama, who seduced a prominent lady; there is no signature, but her handwriting is easily identifiable. If Margarita doesn't abide by her husband's promise, Rodrigo will show him the letters. She begs him to destroy them, but he refuses and leaves, followed by her.

Isabel, who was listening, is attempting to sort things out when a traveler from Palestine is announced. Zulima, in disguise, works the conversation around to the young Aragonese man she knew, recounting his involvement with the queen and how he was forced to flee with a group of bandits, subsequently being killed. Isabel faints, and as Teresa calls for help Zulima leaves. Margarita learns of the visit and that Isabel will not marry, now that Diego is dead. The mother muses upon how marriage without love leads to crime, even after a woman becomes a mother; someone she knows even wears a hair shirt, has been doing penance for fifteen years, and will die in shame. Isabel is thus reminded of what she heard, and agrees to marry Rodrigo de Azagra. She also has letters; Rodrigo will kill her someday. Margarita insists her letters are not innocent, as Isabel's are. The mother, alone, concludes that the girl has to be sacrificed.

In the third act, part one, Teresa helps an unhappy Isabel dress for the wedding. Margarita has gone to care for Jaime Celada, who is wounded. The vespers bell will signal the ceremony, exactly when Diego's time to return expires. Rodrigo arrives declaring he knows

Isabel has letters, and a picture of Diego, because in the house he had an informant. He suggests they can be married in name only, and that she can bring her parents to live with them. Rodrigo will provide any entertainment she wants; in fact, he has changed so much that if Diego returns on time, he can have Isabel. She weeps.

The guests, awaiting the signal, all leave, except Martín. Suddenly Adel appears, asks Marsilla about his son Diego, and is told that he is dead. The Moor inquires what happened to Jaime Celada, disclosing that the Moorish queen came to Teruel in disguise and must have brought the false news; Diego lives. Having saved the amir from an attempted assassination, Diego is rich, but unable to leave for Teruel because of his wounds. He had sent Jaime Celada ahead as his messenger. Margarita arrives, calling her daughter: Jaime has revived and explained the reason for his trip. Before Martín can repeat his news, the bell is heard.

The second part of act III is set in the outskirts of Teruel, where Diego, tied to a tree, curses the thieves who left him there, alone and bound. Zulima happens by, and stops long enough to tell Diego that Isabel is married, explaining that the messenger was wounded and that she, Zulima, gave Isabel the false news. This is her revenge for his rejection. As she leaves, Diego curses her. Adel, Martín, and others find Diego alive, but it is too late for his marriage. He swears to kill Rodrigo.

The scene for the fourth act (the final one in the revised version) is Isabel's room in Rodrigo's house. It is night as Pedro and Martín converse. Zaén and the bandits are in jail, thanks to the Moors who brought Diego's wealth to Teruel. In the confusion, Rodrigo saved Zulima, fittingly, since she made it possible for him to marry Isabel. The house is surrounded by Moors, and Pedro asks Martín to try to send them away so Zulima can escape. With Martín's exit, Teresa appears, screaming; she has seen a ghost going with Rodrigo to the cemetery. Neither Teresa nor Isabel had heard that Diego was alive. Pedro decides to find the two young men; servant and master leave Isabel alone. A Moor who wants to talk to her proves to be Adel, who unveils the tale of Zulima and how she is sheltered there. Isabel's first impulse is to surrender her, but reflecting the queen did it all for love of Diego, she determines her revenge will be greater: she pardons Zulima, and will defend her. With these words Isabel leaves, dismissing Adel, who also exits.

Diego climbs through the window, looking for Isabel. He recalls how seven days before he lay wounded in a fancy bed, telling everybody the story of his courtship. Isabel returns, and the lovers face each other. Isabel is not only surprised, but amazed that Diego dares enter there. She explains her wedding dress as meaning their separation. When he complains of her not keeping her promise to wait for him or become a nun, she says there are reasons, but does not reveal them. Diego protests the secrecy, since he resisted the advances of a queen. She cries, insisting he leave, as her husband's honor is in her hands, leaving her no choice. Diego asks to kiss her on the forehead, which she refuses. Diego reports he left Rodrigo badly wounded in the cemetery, where Azagra mentioned letters and revenge on Margarita and her husband. When Isabel wants to run there to prevent further troubles, Diego interprets it as lack of love for him. He is left alone, gasping, while turmoil and voices are heard closing in; Isabel reappears, taking Diego by the hand, and leads him out of the room. Adel, pursued by a mob, explains that he killed Zulima by order of the king (she planned to kill Diego and Isabel with the poisoned dagger mentioned in the first act). Adel says that Marsilla can corroborate his words. Isabel runs to her mother, and Diego is seen on the floor. Adel thinks Zulima has killed him, but Isabel says that he died of sorrow. Heaven refused to unite them in life, but will do so in the tomb. With these words, she goes toward Diego, asking his forgiveness, but falls before reaching him.

With the 1849 revision some absurdities were left intact, and others added. How could Diego tell time, if it was dark and he had passed out? How can the offender call off a duel? Does noble Margarita repeat the account of her guilt in case Isabel didn't get it the first time? If anything, the mother is even more selfish than in the first version, despite fewer references to her adultery, expressed less bluntly. Margarita goes home instead of to the church, where she knows everyone is, and takes time to tell Martín about Jaime's mission; in turn the gentleman tells her all about Adel's visit. Is all this waste of time to protect the mother? What justifies the further intrigue with Zulima in the house of Rodrigo de Azagra? Too many people pass casually in and out of Isabel's room. In a house surrounded, how can people go in and out so easily? Why are Isabel and Teresa alone uninformed of the return of Diego? Why is Rodrigo not with his bride? How did Diego find his rival but not Isabel, just after the marriage? If Isabel really loves Diego, what kind of revenge is it to defend and forgive Zulima? If a Moor (Adel) could come through the front door of a house surrounded by other Moors, why does Diego enter through a window (conveniently unprotected)? And finally, among unexplained causes, how, really, did Diego and Isabel die?

III *Larra, Macías and Hartzenbusch*

In many Hartzenbusch plays, footnotes or lengthy explanations at the end provide information as to source, historic fact, a date, an explanatory note concerning customs or little-known curiosities of ages past, even the meaning of a word, but there is absolute silence concerning previous editions of *Los Amantes de Teruel*, (Hartzenbusch's version, as well as that of Tirso de Molina which he edited, about which the reader will find information in the chapter dealing with the Spanish classics). This is puzzling considering that the source is a national historic legend, treated many times before Hartzenbusch, who nevertheless guards his sources as if making a conscious effort not to reveal them.

In 1834 Larra staged his *Macías*, so similar to the *Amantes*, according to Hartzenbusch, that he abandoned the idea and stopped writing the play.

The history of *Macías* is interesting. Larra insists in his own comment on the play that his Macías doesn't resemble anyone, dead or alive, in history or fiction. He is a man who loves, and nothing else. This denial is offset by the very real existence of Macías, but first let us see what Larra's connections with him are. In his usual fiery style, the same tone in which he had denied the existence of Macías, Larra claimed that a play was born, referring to *Los Amantes de Teruel*. His exuberant and unbridled style led him to praise not only the drama, but various seamy characters in it, defending the criteria of Hartzenbusch in trying to find a plausible motive for Isabel's marriage to a man she did not love. In this vein, he found her mother's adulterous episode extremely beautiful, and Azagra and Zulima's reckless behavior (aimed at hurting Isabel, no matter how innocent she was), excusable because they also were moved by love. On the other hand, Larra was somewhat offended by the frequent references to Margarita's adultery. Larra blamed the long, aimless speeches on the actors, stating that a short scene, badly performed, could seem endless if recited by actors who did a poor job.

Larra was pleasantly surprised that a new writer would undertake to write a drama based on what he calls in this case a rather well-known national legend, and do it in a different way. A seemingly contradictory statement, not unusual in Larra, is that if the theme were the important thing, Montalbán's play on the same subject would be good, and this one bad, but the former was in Larra's view a poorly constructed tale sprinkled with trivialities, while Hartzenbusch's contained passion and emotion. He goes on to justify everybody's sacrifice, either of self or another, from the separation of Diego and Isabel to her parents' making her unhappy for selfish reasons, and Azagra and Zulima resorting to base behavior which is not rewarded in the end. The rest of the review is dedicated to finding fault with the stage presentation, as if the shortcomings of the play were exclusively the actors' doing. The last part deals with the role of Margarita, with Larra objecting to her references to her guilt in blunt language in front of Isabel. Then the critic elaborates on the destructive power of love, and how it can most certainly kill, as can other emotions. Theories and doctrines can be explained; feelings have to be experienced.

Larra's objection was taken into account by Hartzenbusch in his revision, as the role of the mother was somewhat changed, without eliminating her unfavorable traits altogether, and resulting, if anything, in a more selfish character than in the first version. Hartzenbusch was also criticized, for adding the supposed adultery of Isabel's mother, by Esteban Gabarda, who was working on a documented history of the Amantes which he later published. Hartzenbusch defended his play in these terms:[1]

It is erroneous to believe that someone's memory may be tarnished by a fictitious deed, since fiction, invention, fable, is a drama, not history, so neither praise nor derogatory remarks applied to a historic figure in fiction make him better or worse than he was. Besides, thinking philosophically and justly, the stain, if there is any, would fall on the bad character, extending, at most, to those who procreated and brought him up, and having taken care not to give Isabel's mother a last name there can be no family that would lose anything thereby.

Here Hartzenbusch, in passing, extends the dishonor to Isabel's grandparents. Gabarda's objection as to imputing immoral behavior to Isabel's mother, the defense of Hartzenbusch, and Larra's censure resulted in many revisions, as seen in the 1849 version of *Los Amantes de Teruel,* the most widely known. Larra, however, did not object completely on moral grounds, or even because a lady who is not mentioned in the legend in any specific way was unnecessarily offended, but on his own problems and way of life which were reflected in the way Larra expressed himself. This is where the real Macías has a close connection with the critic.

Macías is a *historic* drama in four acts and in verse by Mariano José de Larra. This is what its author called it, denying any real, historical antecedent. First presented in the Príncipe Theater, September 24, 1834, it was performed five times, and produced again in 1835 and 1836 in Madrid, Barcelona, and Valencia. The setting is Andújar, province of Jaén, in January of 1406, in the palace of the Marquis of Villena. Elvira must wait a year for the return of Macías, a young man in the service of the Marquis Enrique de Villena, but the latter promises her to another trusted servant, Fernán. If she doesn't marry him, her father will disown her, and Elvira herself is the one who imposed the one year term. Nuño, her father, suggests that Macías has probably married in Calatrava. Don Enrique de Villena sent Macías to fight the Moors at Andújar in a spiteful gesture, because the young man took the side of Villena's wife in a divorce suit. Not wishing to kill Macías by his own hand he sends him on a dangerous mission, thereafter allying himself with Fernán to accomplish a more perfect revenge with the projected wedding.

Macías returns without permission to plead with the Marquis in favor of his own plans to marry Elvira, but is scolded for disobeying orders. Elvira faints upon seeing Macías. She is married; her husband's honor is in her keep. Macías asks her to flee with him, and at her refusal talks of challenging Fernán to a duel. When the Marquis arrives, a heated argument ensues, ending in the imprisonment of Macías by order of his master until the duel. Fernán and Elvira argue bitterly, and she threatens to enter a convent if she can't marry Macías, observing she doesn't love Fernán, but owes him respect. Fernán plots Macías's murder, but a servant overhears the plan and warns Elvira, who goes to warn Macías and set him free; she takes him a dagger, to defend himself if necessary, and to kill her if they are discovered before reaching the gates of the city, where she plans to part company with Macías and seek a convent. Fernán arrives in the meantime with a few men; Macías is mortally wounded, and Elvira kills herself with the dagger, which the dying Macías holds out to her.

That play followed Larra's own *El doncel de don Enrique el Doliente* (The Page of don Enrique the Sickly), a novel in forty chapters. Each is preceded by a few verses taken from an old *romance* or ballad. In chapter seventeen, page 341 of the [1913] Paris edition, several troubadours of the *Cancionero de Baena* are mentioned, so Larra must have had access to it. This cancionero was compiled as an offering to King Juan II (1406–1454) by Alfonso de Baena, who included in his collection poetry of fourteenth- and fifteenth-century Spanish troubadours from various parts of Spain, mainly the central regions. Although the *Cancionero de Baena* is not supposed to have been printed until 1851, there are too many similarities and points of contact between *Macías*, the *Doncel*, and certain contents of the *Cancionero* for Larra not to have seen this source.

In the *Doncel*, which also occurs in 1406, Elvira has been married to Hernán for several years. Macías returns and we learn they are cousins, another hindrance to their marriage, if having another husband wasn't enough. Macías loses his life during a battle, and Elvira, demented, visits his tomb, where she dies several years later. Larra reiterates in both novel and drama that his hero is not to be found elsewhere, but then says that Macías's unlucky life belongs to the historian, and his passions to the poet. Larra portrays Macías as he fancies he must have been, including how he must have felt.

Larra, a strong and colorful figure in his own time, is hard to profile without reading practically every available word from biographies to his own reviews. The laborious and absorbing task unfortunately has to be reduced to a couple of lines. A rebel in many ways, while holding steadfastly to some ideas that could have been channeled to his benefit, he fell prey to the wiles of a woman whose indiscretions were quite public, a relationship that posed serious problems for both families, producing in him a hostility toward almost everything, which is reflected in his reviews. If he fancied himself another Macías, however, he missed the mark.

The real Macías, whose poems are reproduced in the *Cancionero de Baena*, lived toward the end of the fourteenth century and beginning of the fifteenth. Gonzalo Argote de Molina, who lived between 1551 and 1596, compiled a curious book titled *Nobleza de Andalucía* (Andalusian Nobility), which includes among other things names of poets from that part of Spain to the exclusion of others. Macías is one of those listed, together with his story, which is as follows: Macías fell in love with a young lady, but his master arranged her wedding to another in his absence. He continued to woo her and she returned his feelings, although it is not specified whether physically or only emotionally. The husband, tired of the situation, had Macías jailed in Arjonilla, where in chains he continued composing verses to his beloved, and sending them to her; how, we are not told. One day as Macías was complaining of his troubled love at his jail window, the irate husband hurled his spear at him, causing his death.

Macías is buried in the church of Santa Catalina in the castle of Arjonilla, with the spear over his casket.

The exaggerated praise and publicity given Larra's review of *Los Amantes de Teruel* by Hartzenbusch is likely more due to the fact that a few days later Larra committed suicide, in a manner similar to the young protagonist of a somber story he published a few months earlier, *Dia de difuntos* (All Saints' Day).

IV *The Legend*

Since it is reproduced in many publications and it has been the inspiration of plays and other literary and artistic expressions, the bibliography of the historic legend of the Amantes de Teruel is considerable, the most complete being *Antonio Serón y su silva a Cintia*, with a prologue by Domingo Gascón, published in Madrid, 1908. The essence is kept in all accounts, pointing to the universal and timeless quality of this exemplary love. The names also remain unchanged, a clear sign of tradition, truth, and respect for such unfortunate young people. Isabel de Segura and Diego Marsilla lived in Teruel, on the same street, since childhood, developing a deep feeling for one another which eventually became love. Isabel's father was opposed to their marriage because Diego was poor, but the young man obtained from the father a period of time during which to acquire enough wealth to be worthy of Isabel. The agreement was that if beyond that allotted time he did not comply, the girl would marry another suitor, a rich man.

For unknown reasons, Diego returned to Teruel the same day the term expired, just when Isabel, forced by her parents and circumstances, married the other man. Diego fell dead at the feet of his beloved. She went to his funeral, to give Diego a kiss she had denied him upon his return, because she had just been given to another, but she also fell dead, upon reaching Diego's body. This happened in 1217.

Another version of the second part of the legend is that Diego went to the wedding feast and, inconspicuously because of the many people present, made his way to the bedroom of the newlyweds, where hidden he witnessed how Isabel asked her husband not to force her to comply with his rights as a bridegroom because the time limit given to her beloved Marsilla should be observed. Azagra was unhappy about her request but respected her wishes. Once he was asleep Diego made his presence known to Isabel, with the consequent shock to her, the denial of a kiss as he asked, and his death. Later she made her husband aware of the situation, whereupon they both took the body of the unfortunate Diego to the doorstep of his father's house, where he was discovered. She died as she approached Diego at the funeral to give him the kiss she had denied him as a parting request.

The oral tradition was reinforced by many written accounts upon the discovery of the caskets containing the bodies of Diego and Isabel, during the rebuilding of a chapel in the church of San Pedro in Teruel, in 1555. A paper, proven to be early enough to be authentic and telling the story of the unfortunate lovers, was found in one of the boxes.

In 1581 Andrés Rey de Artieda published in Valencia the first dramatic version of the historic legend. Titled simply *Los Amantes* (The Lovers), the play begins with the return of Diego to Teruel. At the outskirts of the city the young man tells a companion the story of his love and his apprehension that he may not arrive on time, as indeed happens. The encounter between the long-separated couple takes place at the wedding reception, and at the ball, when Diego dies in the room of the newlyweds. Isabel decides to go to the funeral and kiss Diego, but she falls dead upon reaching him.

Tirso de Molina wrote the second play on the subject[2] in a different way, beginning with the time limit given Diego to make money, the conditions imposed by Isabel's father that she would wed another suitor if the time expired, and the moving scene of Diego's departure. Tirso was faced with the dilemma of filling the gap of several years' wait. This was accomplished by making the rich suitor responsible for sending an emissary to give Isabel the false news of Diego's death, while we actually see him at war. The last act is taken fairly literally from the beginning of the play by Rey de Artieda, with many dramatic resources used by him and some that Tirso developed more fully.

Juan Pérez de Montalbán, in turn, copied Tirso,[3] especially in the second act, but his play is a credit to its author in many scenes. Montalbán adds the intrigue to break Isabel's resistance, carried out by the maneuvering Elena, Isabel's cousin, who loves Diego, and also by the hopeful suitor who must wait until the time limit expires. Montalbán chose the first version of the legend and spared the audience the gruesome, imposing, and agonizing scene of the funeral cortege, having Isabel fall dead right after Diego's demise.

In the eighteenth century there were at least two *melólogos*, spoken dramatic pieces with incidental music to depict the mood, also based on the legend. Emilio Cotarelo y Mori found this type of theater, whose invention he attributed to Rousseau, of unsurpassed boredom. José Subirá made a study of the *melólogo* in Spain in 1949.[4]

Hartzenbusch's play must have sent critics and scholars to their books, both when first presented to the public and when different editions of it were made in subsequent years, given the repeated statement of Hartzenbusch himself, Aureliano Fernández Guerra, and many others to the effect that Montalbán copied Tirso. However, the latter's play was not considered to be authentic, and was judged by Hartzenbusch to be anonymous. It is evident that Pérez de Montalbán's play was the only one being performed until Hartzenbusch produced his version. This is further shown by the fact that the *melólogos* mentioned, while keeping the one unchanged tragic element, the death of the lovers, are inspired by Montalbán's play, as Isabel falls dead shortly after Diego expires, not at the funeral.

One such *melólogo* is an "escena patética" (pathetic scene) titled *La casta amante de Teruel, Da. Isabel de Segura,* (The Chaste Lover of Teruel, Isabel de Segura), written in 1791 by Mariano Nipho. There is no indication of its having been performed. José Subirá found the text, but not the music. He copies as many as forty-seven of the numerous stage directions intended for the only character who speaks, Isabel, as the *melólogo* concerns her death. In a nicely furnished room Diego is lying on a couch, dead. The music underscores the tragic scene. Isabel displays her emotions as she recites her four hundred lines in a variety of ways, with the music depicting her mood during her intervals of silence, until she falls dead.

The other *melólogo,* or "escena trágica lírica" (a tragic lyric scene), entitled *Los amantes desgraciados* (The Unlucky Lovers), is by Luciano Francisco Comella, with music by Blas de Laserna. It was presented in Madrid in the Príncipe Theater on September 16, 1793, and again November 23, 1799. The profusion of instructions concerning staging and the moods to be portrayed by actors and orchestra are extremely interesting and curious, although the public has no way to know about these preliminaries. The four characters are Isabel, her cousin Elena, don Juan, just married to Isabel, and Diego, who arrives during the wedding ball, only to die, followed later by Isabel. Don Juan does not speak at all, Elena and Diego say a few words, the minimum necessary to establish the topic, and the rest is up to Isabel and the accompanying music during her silence.

Comella no doubt took some elements from Montalbán, but they would not appear without having knowledge of Rey de Artieda's play.

Hartzenbusch has nothing good to say about Comella, as can be ascertained from his poem titled *Carta de D. Luciano Francisco Comella* (A Letter from Francisco Luciano Comella), and *Para el album de Pepita González Acevedo* (For the Album of Pepita González Acevedo), mentioned in chapter four of this book. Clearly, Hartzenbusch was familiar with the particular *melólogo* mentioned.[5]

All these works were treated by me at length elsewhere, and as it would take volumes to make a complete study of the controversy over the authenticity of the legend, let me say only that at least five pieces, if not more accounts of the story, were very well known by Hartzenbusch before he wrote a single line. This is reason enough to doubt his claim about the coincidence between Larra's *Macías* and *Los Amantes de Teruel*.

The question raised by Hartzenbusch and others as to how to convince the audience that Isabel, or any other girl, could marry a man she didn't love has no merit in view of the traditional obedience to elders practiced throughout the world and through the ages. A word of honor given by a father, a marriage arranged by parents to ensure the well being of a daughter, the menace of sending a girl to a convent as an alternative, have always weighed heavily, as evidenced by the countless plays in which such instances occur. In the case of Isabel de Segura we find all these elements, with the possible exception of the convent. Isabel herself agreed to marry her wealthy suitor if Diego Marsilla failed to come back before the period of time stipulated by her father. The hope both young lovers had was, naturally, that he would meet the deadline at worst, and most likely beat it. The doubtful circumstance of false notice of Diego's death, facing reality as the time expired, and her word, as well as her father's, having to be honored, must be taken into consideration.

The intrigues involving the penitent mother and Rodrigo de Azagra's attempted blackmail are elements not found in the historic account and, contentions to the contrary notwithstanding, could be detrimental to the real people who bore those names. The wealthy suitor also had his good qualities, because the real one seems to have endured the long wait suffering as much anxiety as Isabel, fearing and expecting the return of Diego, seeing Isabel all this time as something perhaps unobtainable. The fact that she didn't love him did not preclude the possibility of her becoming his wife at a given date; therefore his wait was not an easy one if he could not overcome his feelings in the meantime. Everything seems to indicate that the time given to Diego to make his fortune was six years, since the fateful year was 1217, and it is known that Diego fought in the battle of the Navas de Tolosa, in 1212. However, some accounts give one or two years as the limit, and some dramatic versions of the historic legend give only that much time to the protagonist. This indicates that possibly Diego had returned to Teruel after that battle, and the agreement with Pedro Segura was made later. This, however, is a minor point compared with more important oversights and assumptions made by Hartzenbusch. The cousin in Montalbán's play, Elena, was inspired by a character in Andrés Rey de Artieda's; the same Elena of the *melólogo* by Comella is taken in turn from Montalbán's play, and what Hartzenbusch did was to create his Moorish queen employing a composite of these preceeding characters.

Rey de Artieda, Tirso, and Montalbán set their plays against wars that would justify Diego's leaving Teruel to seek his fortune instead of remaining there, where perhaps his chances would not be as good as being in the service of the king. Hartzenbusch restored the action to its proper date and historic setting, but diluted the story beyond all logic. Taking pains to find the right names and make references to historical details evoking the time, such as recent sects of renegades, battles that took place between 1200 and 1217, and even the name of Teruel's judge for that year, Hartzenbusch sometimes appears to have forgotten that he was not producing a history book but retelling a sad and great story of unfulfilled love. Dramatically it was hardly efficacious to have buried the protagonists in a sea of Moors. Then he invented an adulterous but virtuous and penitent mother, who none the less sacrifices her daughter for selfish motives. The suitor who knows he is going to marry Isabel if Diego doesn't come back on time, in other plays resorts to giving her the false news of his death through a third party, in an effort to accelerate the date of the wedding, not counting on Isabel's waiting for the time to expire. Hartzenbusch plays it two ways: the Moorish queen brings Isabel the false news, while the suitor resorts to blackmail.

In Diego's account to Zulima it is clear that his dedication to Isabel led her father to postpone the wedding to Rodrigo until Diego's time to become rich expired. The girl was promised anyway to the wealthy man. In Rey de Artieda's play the rejected lover is not depicted as jealous, mean, or devious in any way; at the funeral he is the one who tells those present the real cause of Diego's death, and why he doesn't consider it improper behavior that Isabel wanted to kiss the dead man. In fact, the author withholds his name. This follows the episode as related in the old paper found in one of the caskets holding the bodies of Isabel and Diego.

V *Critics and Comments*

Emilio Cotarelo y Mori, to whom Spanish scholars owe so much for his many offerings in different aspects of literature, theater, and music, was not exempt from unfounded concepts or making them on a feeble basis. His contention, when he speaks of the *Amantes*, that a tradition of centuries may be based on a tasteless tale by Boccaccio can be refuted on many levels. Of the paper found next to one of the bodies in 1555, copied by Juan Yagüe de Salas in 1616, Cotarelo says erroneously it is a mishmash of old phrases and words in Castilian, Aragonese, and Catalán. To so describe a story told in uncomplicated language in 1217, is to be blind to the passing of time and history, since Cotarelo was making his observations in 1903.

Cotarelo set out to deny the existence of the real Isabel and Diego by dismissing extant documents as false, without bothering to see most of them or going to Teruel to investigate. By using exclusively literary pieces instead of the tradition of the legend, he locates a series of what he calls anachronisms, upon which he bases his whole theory that the episode was not true. Here Cotarelo fails to see that in each version of the play, Diego is sent to a different war, in a century other than the historic one, precisely because there is no explanation for his delay in returning to Teruel. His arguments are refuted by Jaime Caruana Gómez de Barreda, using Cotarelo's own method, in *Los Amantes de Teruel* (Valencia, Ecir, 1968, fourth edition), an annotated study of the tradition done in his capacity as chronicler of the city of Teruel.

In 1920 George Wallace Umphrey made an edition of Hartzenbusch's play for the Heath Foreign Language Series, with vocabulary and notes. He complains of the unavailability of this particular play for the student, and proposes his edition as an introduction to the study of Spanish Romanticism. The text used is that of Adolf Kressner anthology of Hartzenbusch's plays published in Leipzig in 1887, a collection Umphrey calls definitive. He repeats what others have said about the legend, but his study shows that he read the Rey de Artieda play. Umphrey deems Montalbán's version superior to others, but Hartzenbusch's is at the top. A rather clear definition of Classicism as it differs from Romanticism follows, stressing the tendency of the former movement to convey an idea, while the latter includes the complete person, with feelings and passion rather than logical reasoning. For Spaniards, he adds, Romanticism had a patriotic significance and meant a revival of Siglo de Oro ideas, so it was not a revolutionary movement.

Umphrey contradicts his own views when he finds the ending of *Los Amantes de Teruel* improbable (no matter how historic) and says that to lead to such an ending Hartzenbusch had to be extremely careful in the sketching of his characters and their motivation, where Tirso and Montalbán were only partially successful. Zulima he finds melodramatic, hardly convincing if the play were to appeal to the intellect, but "the improbabilities are willingly ignored by the reader or spectator" (p. xxi). Of the Hartzenbusch revisions Umphrey says the five acts were reduced to four and much of the prose put in poetic form; the diction he found improved, and obscure points clear. Changes in motivation occur, the mother is considerably ennobled, and in all it has lost freshness but gained in literary polish. On page xxviii he praises the unity of action and adds: "In the first version could be seen something of the Romantic tendency to complicate the plot by the introduction of an excessive number of characters and needless episodes, but in its final form the plot is simple and nothing is permitted to interfere with its dramatic development." Mr. Umphrey failed to notice the further complications of the last act, with the house surrounded by Moors, a detail not present in the first version.

Lewis E. Brett included *Los Amantes de Teruel* in his *Nineteenth Century Spanish Plays* (Appleton-Century Crofts, Inc., New York, 1935). After a preliminary biographical sketch, comments on Romanticism, and the general production of Hartzenbusch, Brett suggests the theme of the play was a difficult one because it was not original, but a well-known story. He doesn't take sides on the veracity of the historic legend, but says the three Golden Age plays on the subject are not worth together a fraction of Hartzenbusch's. He continues: "The Golden Age plays bring forward the action to the time of Charles V and his conquest of Tunis (1535), and treat the theme in a manner which represents the art of their time at its worst. Not one of them succeeds in creating the essential atmosphere, in imparting to the lovers a shadow of nobility or passion." One wonders if Mr. Brett had read any of the three plays he so despised. In contrast he praises Hartzenbusch's version highly, stating that this play is the definite version of the legend. Brett critizices those who object to endless revisions as being more apt to harm than improve on the original, and wishes Hartzenbusch had revised more of his plays. An amusing footnote at the beginning of the play reads: "2. *Adel*. In the earlier editions of the play it is made evident that Adel is not, as might appear, the female servant and confidante of Zulima, but rather the *carcelero*, in charge of the prisoners" (p. 125). He assigns to the play the date 1837, an error, since the version used by Brett is in four acts, and the original was in five.

Juan Alcina Franch in his *Teatro Romántico* (Romantic Theater), published in 1968, points out that Hartzenbusch did not create his *Amantes* in a hurry, but very slowly and carefully. He proceeded likewise in the revisions, leaving the 1849 edition with less prose and minus a few useless characters. Alcina calls attention to certain changes; for instance, Azagra doesn't tell Margarita about Roger de Lizama's death; the mother in turn lets Isabel know about her guilt in an indirect way, and Isabel pardons Zulima in what Allison Peers, as quoted by Alcina, deems an extremely beautiful scene. Alcina states that a first draft of *Los Amantes de Teruel* by Hartzenbusch was all in prose, and that the work stopped when he noticed the similarity to *Macías*. At the suggestion of the actor Juan Lombia, who starred in the play in its first performance, Hartzenbusch alternated prose and poetry. Although Alcina's evaluation of the play is systematic and original in its approach, he included some of the bibliographical data without checking items quoted, as he calls Andrés Rey de Artieda *Francisco*; this is hardly a typographical error, since Alvaro Gil de Albacete made the same mistake in his edition of the play in volume 113 of Clásicos Castellanos, 1954, page xv.

Alcina's edition is that of 1850, which contains at least two revisions since the original play of 1836, but attributes (according to unidentified sources) the creation of Zulima to the suggestion of the aforementioned actor Lombia, to fill the void of Diego's delay. To justify Isabel's marriage to a man she did not love, the episode of the mother's own history was invented, giving her character great importance, as mothers are very rare in the Spanish Theater of the Siglo de Oro as well as in the Romantic period. Alcina praises the deviation from the norm in the drama of Hartzenbusch's times: death due to love is from natural causes, not by suicide, as was then the fashion. Martín's only justification for being in the play, Alcina believes, is to give his son the news of Isabel's wedding. He conjectures that the duel that doesn't take place between Pedro and Martín makes the latter's presence on stage plausible. Margarita and her guilty past are deemed to foreshadow a repetition of events in the future of Isabel. Rodrigo's aiding Pedro against Roger de Lizama and the subsequent intrigue force Isabel to accept the marriage. Alcina finds evil even in Marsilla's desperation, when he exclaims that adversity breaks the ties of man with life and virtue, and he wants to avenge upon others his misfortune.

Salvador García published an edition of the first version of *Los Amantes de Teruel* in 1971. He seems to like everything about the way Hartzenbusch rendered the story, from the many intrigues to justifying the actions of Zulima and Rodrigo, because love motivates them. Honor moves Margarita to force Isabel to marry as if voluntarily. García observes that Diego doesn't leave Teruel in search of adventures, but is forced to do so by the circumstances. In no way is this different from the other versions, so it seems unnecessary to bring this item up. He is surprised by the loyalty Isabel and Diego keep to each other, nothing new either. In this vein García's evaluation of the play suggests at times that he has read no other play on the subject matter, in spite of the abundant bibliographical material he quotes. At least, the text of the five original acts is made available by him, as opposed to the more widespread revision of 1849 in four acts.

It is noteworthy that none of these critics brings out the fact that there seems to be no pattern, no reason for alternating prose and verse, as was done in other plays of the times. Occasionally the verse suits a scene very well, but there is no perceptible guiding principle or method. Hartzenbusch filled in with his imagination the only gap in the story: what caused the delay of Diego Marsilla. However, the shock of Diego's return and the forced wedding of Isabel left no room for the former's giving the obviously lengthy explanation. The double death occurring in such a short time was the event that made the extraordinary story famous. The tragic end jolts everyone, but it is practically impossible to retrace steps known only to those in the middle of the problem; only a partial reconstruction of the main events is possible.

In the case of the *Amantes de Teruel* the loyalty, constancy, pure love conceived in childhood, the sensitivity of both protagonists, their observance of human and divine laws, are exemplary. The practically unendurable and purposeful absence of Diego, the anguished wait of Isabel, caught in the dilemma of filial obedience, courted by a suitor she did not want, and the fulfillment of a word of honor, attest to qualities instilled in young people by tradition, moral parents, religious teachings, and respect for the elders. Hartzenbusch in his alterations, must have fallen prey to his eagerness to produce at last a play that would please the rebellious contemporary writers. Rather than emphasizing their moral fiber, as well as the deep feeling and suffering of Diego and Isabel, Hartzenbusch not only filled the gap of Diego's delay, but invented various unfortunate social sins.

The opinion of the critics, especially the one who was then at the top, Larra, triggered a number of reactions. Many agreed with Larra, and the author decided to alter the more sensitive areas. Some disapproved of the handling of the story as a melodrama, imputing bad traits to some of the characters that were not so described in the original story. Others, showing callousness or lack of historic and dramatic perception, accepted the last version, considerably re-touched, as the only one in existence. A bit of research would prove that Boccaccio, credited by some as a source for the plot, was born much later than the protagonists, the account of whose misfortune could have easily traveled to Italy at a time when a good part of its territory was under Aragonese domination. Boccaccio, besides, is not known for his scruples when it comes to appropriating material.

If a play is to be considered on its own merits, always subject to the particular slant of a scholar, the play itself provides the proving ground. When it depicts an historic event, however, the author should reflect it accurately. Conversely a critic or scholar has the duty to see whether justice has been done or if the historicity is merely a springboard for relaying a message. Often a happening is placed against an historic background that only provides the atmosphere, while some peripheral episode becomes the focal point. Such is the case when the story of the unfortunate lovers of Teruel is transported to another century, against the background of a war that could account for the long absence of Diego. The ill-starred love is central, not the historic times when it took place. Hartzenbusch respected the date, but altered what should have been left intact. There are also those who compare the greatness of the love of Isabel and Diego to the "unsurpassed" story of Romeo and Juliet. Their situations are quite different, since the latter couple did not even consult their feuding families, but found an officious priest who showed very little common sense in marrying them without first going to their parents. Romeo and Juliet consummated their make-do marriage, and later, in an effort to flee together, which failed, committed suicide by mistake. Isabel and Diego, the lovers of Teruel, did nothing improper, re-sorted to no subterfuge to bypass the authority of their parents, and died for each other, all in a very Christian way. Their example, although as involuntary as the death of Romeo and Juliet, is moral in every way.

CHAPTER 4

Poetry

H ARTZENBUSCH'S poetry is found primarily in *Obras. Poesías*
(Colección de escritores castellanos líricos, Madrid, Yenes,
1887, Tomo 1 (Works. Poetry. Collection of Castillian Lyric Writers).
This collection contains sixty-five poems. *Ensayos poéticos y artículos
en prosa, literarios y de costumbres,* Madrid, Yenes, 1843 (Poetic
Essays and Prose, Literary and Costumbristic Articles) contains only
twenty-one, of which one, "Los esposos en Panticosa" (The Married
Couple at Panticosa), is not included in the larger collection. On page
seventy-nine one other poem has a different title, "Otro pintor ciego"
(Another Blind Artist), but is the same in content as "Versos para un
album" (Verses for an Album). Only twelve poems are found in the
German edition of Hartzenbusch's selected works, and these are
included in the larger collection, except for one in praise of Alberto
Lista.

In order to give a representative sampling of Hartzenbusch's
poetry, the largest collection of his poems will be utilized, including
his translations, since in other volumes only a few are found. My
classification of said poetry does not attempt to be erudite, but
informative, to better form an idea of the man and his writings.

As an important part of a portrait being painted in many sections
that eventually resolve into a whole, the poetry reveals traits of the
personality of the author. It has been most rewarding to find such
things as the source of Hartzenbusch's Catholicism, his quest for the
Germanic elements in his psychological makeup, his inability to cut
loose from the Spanish essence he sometimes despises but at others
claims as a wonderful heritage.

Hartzenbusch writes verse with great ease; as in his plays, the
terms he uses may not be refined or unfailingly adequate to the image
or thought conveyed, but rhyme is achieved. Carelessness or haste to
keep the verse flowing is suggested by the meter he uses; no
particular subject is accorded a given verse form, and often more than

one or two meters are used within the same poem for no evident reason. It is puzzling that a man whose facility in verse form enabled him to write in a seemingly effortless manner would not muster more select terms of language or the adequate mixture to write beautiful poetry when commissioned to do so. My observations along these lines were also confirmed in the prologue to his fables, where he expresses dissatisfaction with his verses. Emotions, observations, historical events, and comments are among topics elaborated in his poetry.

As examples we have "El amante desdeñado" (The Rejected Lover), wherein a man complains of hopeless love beneath the window of his beloved. She speaks the words he longs to hear to another man. "La muerte" (Death) is a work wherein the poet ponders the life of the body, human resistance to leaving this world, and wonders about life and death. The degree of force or beauty varies when an historical event is the subject. "El alcalde Ronquillo" (Mayor Ronquillo) offers an excerpt taken from accounts of the death of the bishop of Zamora, Acuña. In jail, he complains of the injustice done by Charles V to the Comuneros[1] and defends those who rebel against the Belgian dominance. Ronquillo enters and, in turmoil, his subordinates refuse to touch the bishop. The mayor himself executes the holy man. This is an unpleasant poem, both in contents and in language, as is "Isabel y Gonzalo," a legend in three parts, dealing with the illegitimate daughter of Enrique II and her lover, Gonzalo, whom the king opposes.

The inauguration of a building also offers a pretext for the facility with which Hartzenbusch wrote in verse, as seen in "A la inauguración del Instituto Español" (To the Inauguration of the Spanish Institute), "La estátua de Felipe IV y el busto de don Pedro Calderón de la Barca hablan del Teatro Real en las siguientes décimas" (The Statue of Philip IV and the Bust of Pedro Calderón de la Barca Speak of the Royal Theater in the Following Verses); and "En la inauguración de la Escuela Central de Agricultura" (On the Inauguration of the Central School of Agriculture). The latter contains some dutiful praise to the queen, as does another poem commemorating her placing the first stone for the building of museums and national library. Two more about theaters and audiences have the peculiarity of being done in archaic Spanish.

Some treat inherently antipoetic themes, such as critizicing wo-men, deploring the style of hats, or making a play on words. In this vein "Ellas y ellos" (Women and Men) asks which sex is morally better; a footnote reveals how woman transmits all evils to man. "A una romántica" (To a Romantic Woman) is a short piece in which Hartzenbusch tells a woman, unsympathetically, to stop reading and pining; she should be sewing, or taking care of plants. Another suggestion is that she change her dress so she won't be taken for a salmon when she is a hake and that she eat a lot.

The poetry includes some translations and imitations from foreign authors, such as Metastasio, Schiller, Alessandro Manzoni, and Bengenbach. Several poems deal with the Napoleonic invasion of Spain (1808) and with the war in Africa. Later, the aging poet reflects upon the past and the mark of time, as in "A Juan su pícara memoria" (To Juan, His Mischievous Memory), "La vida del hombre" (Man's Life), "En un album" (In an Album), and "La dicha" (Happiness). In "Epigrama" (Epigram), the author notes he does not like to see a wedding, and when he sees a funeral he thanks God, grateful he is not the deceased. Sad happenings such as the death of a friend, a public figure, or an actress retiring from the stage, are among other themes, some commissioned to Hartzenbusch.

While some pieces praise Lope de Vega, Calderón, Alberto Lista, and other writers, there are two vicious attacks on Tirso de Molina and Luciano Francisco Comella.[2] In "La medianía de ingenio" (Mediocre Talent) Hartzenbusch recognizes his own shortcomings. This long poem seems to have been written after one of his plays was not well received.

While Hartzenbusch finds it difficult to praise women or describe their beauty, as proven by his inability to say anything specific about Julia, Eladia, and Laura in as many poems (wherein he says only he can't do them justice), there is a definite sensitive note in other compositions. One such is "El pintor ciego. A Esquivel. Soneto" (A Sonnet to the Blind Artist Esquivel); his plight is that, having lost his eyesight, he has not lost his talent, but cannot use it. Two poems to the baths of Panticosa praise its waters, which retard death. It seems that Hartzenbusch took his sick wife there in hope of her recovery. "Al busto de mi esposa" (To a Bust of My Wife) is directed to the marble bust of his first wife, enclosed in glass.

The theme of marriage is given a macabre twist in "La cama de matrimonio" (The Double Bed, 1854). Where is the carpenter going? To make a bed for himself and Florentina, his bride-to-be. Her wedding dress has not come out quite right; it looks more like a shroud. The girl says she does not feel well; maybe it will serve her soon. Where is the carpenter going? To make a bed without legs, the last one all of us have; Florentina is dead.

"Un enfermo a un vaso de agua" (A Sick Man to a Glass of Water) expresses the patient's gratitude for the relief water brings him, but also blesses the thirst which brings him a good thing to make him better. Turning to the divine, the poet states that only heavenly virtue will quench man's thirst. Hartzenbusch may have been unaware how his observations could give cause for reflection. This poem can spark a meditation that redeems some of the author's less fortunate material. This poem raises the larger question of what happens when thirst is present and the water is not available. Worse yet is the case in which the water or the glass are denied the thirsty person. Supposing the glass or container is the human being; what good is it, if the water he craves will always be out of reach?

"La casa de la madre" (The Mother's House) is a poem placed at the end because of its importance. I had been puzzled while doing research for this book by one aspect of Hartzenbusch as a writer. While critical of his approach to many subjects, I detected a constant theme: his faith. This poem reveals not only that I was right, but the source of this peculiar axis. These verses, inspired or triggered by the rebuilding of a sanctuary near Sevilla by the Duke and Duchess of Montpensier, are connected by the author with the birthplace of his mother. Because of limitations as a versifier I will give a prose summary of this very sensitive poem.

Hartzenbusch saw his mother, dead at twenty-two, in the casket, dressed in black and white, hands crossed, surrounded by lights. He was only two years old; that was the last time he saw her, before he could understand such things as death. Later at a church he saw people praying before a sad and beautiful figure of a woman surrounded by the light of many candles, dressed in black and white, with her hands crossed and seven daggers in her chest. "That is my mother" exclaimed the child. A young man turned to him and said "no," but an old lady told him "yes," explaining to him that she was the mother of all, and her name was Mary, also the name of Hartzenbusch's mother. The child fused in his mind the two Marys, and even as an adult he kept that image.

The impact Hartzenbusch received as a child remained in full force as he grew, because his young mind perceived a sad experience which he could not fully understand, and stayed with him in a pure light that nothing could change. The mysteries of religion, life and death, fate and the will of God, are tinged in some way by the faith Hartzenbusch shows throughout his works. This aspect gained reality upon finding this poem, from which the root of his Catholicism stems. The loss of his father, his young first wife, and his second spouse in his old age, were closer to our author in the sense that these beloved people had major roles in his life; for better or worse, he lived with them for years, and each death was a very sad experience. Only his mother was for a short time near him physically, but her impact in his life stems from the day he saw her in the bier and his association of that image with the similar one seen in church, the confusion created in his mind, and the inability to feel emotions at that tender age as compared to those that came gradually to him as he grew.

CHAPTER 5

Fables

I *The Fable Writers*

THE second volume of Hartzenbusch's selected works, published
in 1888, contains fables printed at different times, ranging from
1843 to 1863, and others published in a fragmentary manner. In the
preface, the author acknowledges that his fables are not original, not a
product of his imagination except in those cases where he thought it
best to change or retouch the story. As in other instances he gives no
clue as to what he has done with the original, whereas at other times
there are lengthy notes. The first name mentioned in connection with
his book of fables is that of Félix María Samaniego, of whom he says he
adds to his translations so there will be more in Spanish. He avoids
Tomás de Iriarte because he only dealt with literary matters, but
expresses his admiration for Ramón de Campoamor. Hartzenbusch
paves the way for his version of fables, citing the example of the king
who had a statue of Flora, cast in bronze, in the center of a garden
pond in all his palaces, and the controversy that arose when he put a
sitting, lead Flora in a new palace. Another example is that of the
architect Maximum, who built wonders of refuse and odds and ends,
but when Minimum tried the same thing, he was not admired.
Hartzenbusch contends that experiments must be accepted, not
merely criticized; he notes that his predecessors were not original,
naming among others La Fontaine, Phedro, Babrio, and a few
Spaniards. He claims to have given new form to old fables and others'
thoughts, ending with a few lines from Calderón de la Barca's *Nadie
fíe su secreto* (Let Nobody Confide His Secret):

> Remendaba con sigilo
> Sus calzones un mancebo:
> Yo, que le acechaba, vilo,
> Y pregunté: ¿Qué hay de nuevo?—
> Y él respondió:—Sólo el hilo.

Meaning: "A young man was mending his trousers. I was watching and asked him: 'What's new?' He answered: 'Only the thread.' "

Let us see what his predecessors did. Félix María Samaniego was born in La Guardia, in the Basque provinces, October 12, 1745 and died in 1801. Of a wealthy family, after much study and travel, plus tending to the administration of his possessions, he was mayor of the city of Tolosa. Cultured, and given to artistic endeavors, he published his first collection of moral fables in 1781. Contemporary of another renowed Spanish fabulist, Tomás de Iriarte, Samaniego dedicated to him the third book of his fables. The main difference between Hartzenbusch and Samaniego is that the latter was the first Spaniard who, in his own words, stooped to write such delightful moral lessons in a simple yet adequate language for children to learn, even if by rote. Not unlike La Fontaine, he translated fables from many languages and sources, to make them available in Spanish as a contribution to a sound moral upbringing. Thus the warnings, teachings, and thoughts passed down from generation to generation were enriched by Samaniego's contribution. He studied the premise of the fable and read many, hoping to take as examples Aesop, Phedro, and La Fontaine, but he found the first too dry and exact to do him justice in Castillian verse; the second had borrowed very heavily from others, adding so much of his vocabulary that he could not be used as a good model; as for La Fontaine, his fables lacked the directness and conciseness necessary to reach the young intellect. Samaniego does not claim to have achieved the ideal formula, but his early discoveries were foremost in his mind, and he tried to apply his own rules whenever possible. He went back to the earliest originals, bypassing more modern versions in an effort to render into clear Spanish the moral teachings of Aesop, changing words as necessary, altering the didactic purpose, but without touching the main core.

Hartzenbusch in no way follows this example. Where he differs from Samaniego is that he emulated the latter but not in the same way, and incurred criticism when trying to reuse material that in the eyes of others should be left alone.

Tomás de Iriarte was born September 18, 1750, in Puerto de la Cruz, Tenerife (Canary Islands), one of many children of a military man. He studied under one of his brothers, a Dominican friar, and moved to Madrid in 1764. He continued his studies and soon became interested in literature and the theater in all its forms. He worked as a translator and occupied different posts, such as archivist, music teacher and others suitable to his talents, while moving in political, diplomatic and nobility circles. He also published the results of his erudition and writing talent at different times and touching various subjects. In 1782 Iriarte published his *Fabulas literarias* (Literary Fables). Several plays followed, including the curious type of the *melólogo*, discussed in chapter three in reference to the *Amantes of Teruel*. He died in Sanlúcar September 17, 1791. Iriarte's fables, literary, as he called them, are original, based upon moral lessons both Christian and civil, aiming to contribute to man's well-being by observing moral laws, as well as helping him move in the world in peace with others. Quite different from Samaniego's fables in length and purpose, Iriarte was a second example of a Spanish writer who delved into the genre as such, paving the way for Hartzenbusch, who undertook to translate mainly from the German.

The type of moral teaching found in fables was far from new in Spain in the eighteenth century; precedents are the many sayings and examples found in the *Cancioneros*, collections of popular proverbs and similar writings, and the timeless book of examples compiled by the Infante Don Juan Manuel under the name of *El Conde Lucanor*. Other examples can be found that precede considerably any collection of fables imitated or brought to Spain from foreign lands.

One more fabulist, admired by Hartzenbusch, was his contemporary Ramón de Campoamor, a poet and politician. Born in 1817, in Navia, Asturias he died in 1901. As a reaction against his strict religious education, which took him to the verge of becoming a Jesuit, Campoamor studied medicine for a time, but science did not answer his questions, and he turned to law and politics. He published poems of different kinds and several books on politics. His poetry differs from that of his contemporaries in that he purposely tried to stay away from exaggerations and flourishes, achieving a very personal touch which, as his themes, are free of influences of other writers, old or modern, national or foreign. His definition of art is that it is idealist when the image is applied to ideas, realist when it deals with things, and naturalist when it does not go beyond what the five senses perceive. The fifty-seven fables included in his complete works are divided into five categories: literary, political, religious, moral, and philosophical. As examples of the political we find "Oficios mutuos" (Mutual Occupations), which deals with how today's executioner is tomorrow's condemned man, and vice versa. "Percances" (Incidents), also on politics, shows how a throne can be a scaffold, and a scaffold at times is a throne. In the philosophical vein, "No siempre el bien es fortuna" (Something Good Is Not Always

Good Luck) deals with the captive bird that has a taste of freedom, and once back in its cage, sings no more. (The poet doesn't mention the dangers of being outside one's own element). "Yendo a más venir a menos" (Advancing and Suddenly Falling Below), also philosophical, is about the deception of finding one's career cut short. An example of a moral fable, "La carambola" (Carambole), illustrates how the harm we do to someone may be returned to us through a third person. Campoamor defines his requirements for a good fable, stating that the action should maintain interest, the protagonist should act according to his natural qualities and character, the plot must be uncomplicated, the language clear, and the result should be a moral teaching.

Hartzenbusch's approach differs from that of Samaniego, Iriarte, and Campoamor. Primarily, he translates from Pfeffel, Gellert, Lichtwehr, Hagedorn, Gleim, Ramler, Leibeskind, French Collections, and, above all, Lessing. Thirty of these are included in the 1843 edition of miscellaneous works. Because of their length, many of Hartzenbusch's fables defy transposition. Some have a short explanation at the end, done by the author himself, because their contents are not always fully intelligible. Often they are alien to Spanish concepts and culture, being filtered and translated from the German, so that only the gist in clear Spanish makes sense. Others, expressed in very good Castilian, are short, and make their point with no trouble. Some, however, seem to be mere exercises in translation with no message, or else one that is lost in the process. At times the author uses this vehicle to express grievances, personal or borrowed, or to rail against other writers, so that there is not sufficient reason to call it a fable, because it contains no teaching. For no apparent reason, Hartzenbusch uses the name of Jupiter to mean God in some fables that have to do with man per se, but not with mythology. Some examples are taken from well-known Spanish writers (he gives only the name, not the source). The numbers correspond to no visible order, and are not consistent in different editions. A slight change in title often means repetition, and it is clear that in his zeal to translate, Hartzenbusch did not sift.

II *Gotoldo Efrain Lessing's Fables*

Hartzenbusch opines that Lessing differs from fabulists of other countries in that his moral is there for the reader to find, implicit but not explicit, so that a teaching can be extracted whether moral, literary, religious, or political, applicable to each country and different epochs. Pinpointing the moral teaching, it only serves once; *omitting it*, he says, it can be used repeatedly. Thus Lessing's fables are more suitable for adults than for children. Hartzenbusch hastens to add that the same can be said of Iriarte, whose fables are literary. While Iriarte's fables are specifically literary, Lessing's fall into no identifiable category, especially after Hartzenbusch's deviations from the original so they would not sound strange in Spanish. In case the meaning is vague, many have explanatory notes provided by Hartzenbusch (who versified Lessing's prose fables). As a sample he includes thirty, some of which follow. [1]

"El ruiseñor y la calandria" (The Nightingale and the Lark) offers the example of two songbirds, one of which complains that if the other sings too far above, his song cannot be understood; in this way he chides poets who write in a lofty manner. In defense of the modern we find "Le estátua de bronce" (The Bronze Statue). A bronze statue melted by fire was recast by a modern sculptor; the only praise he received was for some to say that it came from good material. The explanatory note says that if something modern is good, it must be a copy.

"El racimo" (The Bunch of Grapes) deals with an envied poet, who is compared to the fox trying in vain to reach a bunch of grapes; finding the enterprise impossible, the fox said the grapes were green. A bird heard, and tasted one; it was good, and soon a hundred birds picked clean the bunch of grapes. "El arco" (The Bow) tells us of a hunter who carved and so refined a bow that it broke when he tried to use it. The moral of the story, as he explains, is that to file and smooth excessively robs energy; refined culture lacks strength. In "Los Gorriones" (The Sparrows) the poet presents a church rebuilt. The many sparrows that used to live there could not find their holes and left, the message being that when there is a social reform the parasites are out, and they think without them the world cannot function.

The author employs irony in "El cordero protegido" (The Protected Sheep) as two dogs fighting to guard a sheep end up killing it. Modifying the well-known fable "El cuervo y la zorra" (The Crow and the Fox), Hartzenbusch relates that a butcher poisoned a piece of meat to rid himself of a neighbor's cat; a crow picked it up and flew it to a tree to eat it. A fox came by and praised the crow who, flattered, spread its wings in flight. The meat fell, the fox ate it, and the poison went to work. The obvious message is that it would be useful if this happened to flatterers. Yet another moralizing attempt is found in

"Jupiter y la oveja" (Jupiter and the Lamb), wherein the lamb complains of being defenseless, but concludes that the power to hurt brings out the evil in others, so it prefers to suffer. Jupiter blessed the lamb. In another animal fable, "Los dos ciervos" (The Two Deer), an old deer reminisces about the time when rifles were not yet invented. A younger deer opines it must have been good in those days; not so, the former explains: there were bows and arrows. In every epoch, there are means to hurt the weaker.

"Los beneficios" (The Benefits) presents a bee who asked a wise man if anyone gave more than she did. He answered that the sheep did, because honey is sweet but the bee may sting; the sheep gives wool. Hartzenbusch adds the note that utilitarian things are more important. "El caballo de ajedrez" (The Chess Knight) retells the incident of two boys playing chess with an incomplete set who substituted a knight with a pawn, marking it to distinguish it from the other pawns. The others protested, but the boys said it was just as worthy to them. The author explains that all aristocracies are the same: that of utility is as worthy as that of birth.

III *Other Fables*

In an orthodox admission of relativity, Hartzenbusch in "El niño en alto" (A Child up High) relates that a child upon a chair said proudly he was a giant. Get down, he was told, and you will be a dwarf. In "El muchacho y la vela" (The Boy and the Candle) a related principle is illustrated: A child said to a candle: "I want to shine like you someday." The candle answered: "My fate is anguish and smoke; I shine, but shining I am spent."

"La alacena" (The Cupboard) presents the prototypical travelers who spend the night in a farmhouse. During the night there is a tremendous sound like a storm. One man asks the other to look out to see if it has rained. The other man, in the dark, opens doors not to the outside, but to a pantry where cheese is kept. His report is that it is not too damp, but smells of cheese. Hartzenbusch comments that, blindly, some people criticize because they are looking in the wrong place. Moralizing of a similar nature is found in "El escritor y el ladrón" (The Writer and the Thief), wherein a common thief does not bother to conceal what he takes, but a writer takes the trouble to disguise what he steals from another; otherwise it is not worth it.

"Los caribes" (The Caribes) presents an old gentleman who visited a Caribbean island to study it, but the natives ate him. They found that despite all his knowledge he was insipid and tough. The fabulist tells us that no preaching sinks into those whose only guide is the stomach. Cynicism seems to increase in "Los cuclillos" (The Cuckoos), wherein the bird born of an egg left to hatch in a strange nest for other birds to care for does not thank them; that is the way parents and pupils pay the teacher, the moralist says. Alluding to a classical title and topic in "La verdad sospechosa" (Suspicious Truth), Hartzenbusch portrays a tough man hit by a bullet who says he is not dead, but nobody believes him.

"El látigo" (The Whip) gives a new turn to an old theme: a child steals from his mother's spinning wheel. She notices, finds a whip made with the scraps he stole, and punishes him with it. Not too originally, Hartzenbusch says that vice brings its own punishment.

"El espejo y el agua" (The Mirror and the Water) is a fable in which the mirror and the water argue that the mirror, being hard, reflects things faithfully, but the soft water only partially. The direct reprimand hurts, while mild scolding makes people mend their ways.

"El nadador" (The Swimmer) offers more practical, albeit strange, moralizing: a young man who went to swim in the Tagus River almost drowned. A friend saved him, and he said: "I am not getting into the water again until I learn how to swim." In "La lluvia de verano" (Summer Rain) Lucas, caught without proper clothing, is soaked, as is the gun of a robber. In our author's version of "El diamante y el cristal" (The Diamond and the Glass), an unpolished diamond and a piece of glass fell on the road. The diamond was stepped upon and buried in the dust, while the bright glass was picked up by travelers. The moral seems to be that merits are put down if not touted. "El peral" (The Pear Tree) presents an opposite case: a boy hurled a rock at a pear tree, which responded by giving him a pear. The good souls return a favor for harm received. Changing his symbolism in "La escala" (The Scale of Proportion) the author tells us that a martin eats a mosquito, because he is small and the bird is big; *a milano* (bird of prey) eats the martin and offers the same excuse; an eagle eats the *milano* for the same reason, and a hunter kills the eagle. A bad action, the author says, has to be paid for at some point; after all, the mosquito was sucking the blood of the hunter.

Turning to women and marriage, we find several fables worth noting. "La novia serpiente" (The Serpent Bride) tells how many girls seem sweet, but the minute they get married they show their true disposition, that of a serpent. "La esposa modelo" (The Model Wife), "El viudo" (The Widower), "Andrés Morugo," and "La viuda del malabar" (The Juggler's Widow), respectively, deal with paying lip service to a dear one upon the verge of death, but not being willing to trade places, burying a wife in her best clothes, or wishing to be with one's mate either in Paradise or in Hell. "Escena de segundas nupcias" (Scene of a Second Marriage) seems to be a possible fragment of a larger story: a father asks his daughter from his first marriage what she leaves him as farewell, since she is going to lose her life. She answers she leaves him her blessing, and curses her step-mother, who causes her to die.[2]

Some more dubious moralizing is found in the next three fables: "Despacito y buena letra" (Slowly But Surely), concerns a shepherd who hurriedly negotiates a rugged mountain pass on his way to a monastery to hear Mass; he trips, falls, hurts his head, and misses Mass anyway. To hasten thoughtlessly does not pay, the author says. "La anciana indevota" (The Nondevout Old Lady) cites the example of an old woman who prayed to every saint in church except St. Michael, claiming that the devil had frightened her. The priest finally extracted the truth from her: the image was made from a cherry tree, which is what she saw, not the saint. The priest tells her we must not look upon anybody as they were, but as they are now. The third one, a strange mixture of suggested religions, is "El dedo índice de la mano izquierda" (The Index Finger of the Left Hand). The king of Persia set out to find a wife by looking only at the left index finger of the girls. Ester won because hers was pricked from sewing. According to Hartzenbusch that is how a woman with good hands is valued among Christians.

A claim that if one threatens, he may end up with nothing is made at the end of "El barbero" (The Barber), wherein a gentleman complained to a barber of his tardiness. The barber observed that if he did not like to wait he might learn to shave himself. The gentleman reacted, saying he would let his beard grow and dispense with his services. Many more fables on a variety of topics are found, some of which include "A good marriage is heaven on earth," "A father should not ask his son to make a sacrifice he himself is not willing to make," and "In the words of a horsefly, if you smell like a donkey you must be one." Whatever prompted our next and final example, Hartzenbusch would have done well upon occasion to heed its teaching:

> "El fiscal" (The Judge):
> Proofreading something
> a certain picky judge

tried to correct by his own hand
three errors he found made by the scribe,
light orthographic mistakes.
He scratched what was wrong,
but so clumsily or with such anger
that he made three holes in the paper.
Upon seeing it ruined
he tore it up and threw it away,
mixed with weeds.
There are censors of such gentle mood
that they cannot correct without destroying. [3]

CHAPTER 6

Other Writings

I Short Stories

IN the selected works of Hartzenbusch, published in Leipzig in 1863, are nine short stories, as well as the poetry, fables, and other works already discussed in previous chapters. Page 155 contains a vocabulary of old or archaic Castilian for the better understanding of two tales written in that form. Some words can be understood in context in these stories, but others are an obvious effort on the part of the author to flaunt his erudition. The first title, *La hermosura por castigo* (Beauty as Punishment), deals with a blind but very beautiful princess who obtained her eyesight on one condition, that she could not see the thing she loved the most until she died; only then did she see her own face. Next is *Palos de Moguer*, explaining how that town in southern Spain got its name. Traditionally, husbands gave their wives an annual beating (*palos* meaning blows in this case) because of a silly argument between a man and his wife, resulting in all the women taking her side and all the men his, ending in a general free-for-all. *La reina sin nombre* (The Queen without a Name) is labeled a Visigothic chronicle of the seventh century; it offers a variation, in eight chapters, of problems expounded in *La ley de raza* (The Race Law), a play discussed in chapter two, and other period plays by Hartzenbusch. Each chapter is prefaced by verses from one of his plays; there is also an appendix, conclusion, footnotes, and references to history books.

La novia de oro (The Bride of Gold) and *Mariquita la pelona* (Little Mary the Bald), both written in old Castilian, were composed by Hartzenbusch to amuse a lady whose hair had to be cut because of illness. The first tale deals with Solomon, rich but of poor intellect, who takes counsel from a poor man, Babieca (name of the horse of the Cid). The moral is that a woman who spends her husband's fortune is bad, and ends up badly. Mythological, astronomical, and would-be humorous names used are altered in a derogatory way which the author has used in other instances, notably in some plays. The second tale is labeled a chronicle of the fifteenth century, and revolves about a girl who cut her hair to help her father. A footnote informs the reader that Hartzenbusch received two analogous pieces after the publication of *Mariquita*. These are also published. The similitude ends with the subject of hair woven somehow into the story; *Miriam la trasquilada* (Miriam the Sheared) is placed in the times of the Old Testament, and *Doña Mariquita la Pelona* (Miss Little Mary the Bald) is purportedly a biographical letter from an unknown person. Finally, *La locura contagiosa* (The Contagious Madness) is labeled a seventeenth-century anecdote concerning Cervantes and his writing of the *Quijote*, while the last story, *La deuda olvidada* (The Forgotten Debt), relates the life of Alfonso Zamora, who suffered from insomnia; it would not go away until he paid all his debts. When he paid his debt to God, he died.

II *Articles on Several Topics*

With poetic essays we find prose articles, literary and costumbristic, as published by Yenes in 1843. Some labeled literary fall specifically into the category of drama, as different aspects of it are really the subject. For a contest in the Lyceum on January 31, 1841, Hartzenbusch wrote "Examen del teatro de D. Ramón de la Cruz" (An Evaluation of the Theater of Ramón de la Cruz). Dated simply 1839 is a brief biography and an account of the works of Dionisio Villanueva y Ochoa, known as Dionisio Solís, a poet born in Córdoba in 1774. There is also an article on the Spanish tragedy, dated 1838; another concerning the dramatic unities was written in March 1839, and one titled simply "Notes" was read at the Atheneum, and bears the date February 25, 1842. This is a speech answering the question of whether, given the state of literature, politics, and moral climate of Spain, there could be a national theater, and if so what should dramatic poets do to achieve it.

"Costumbristic articles" is not the best term to translate *artículos de costumbres*, since even in Spanish the phrase stands for a concept rather than for the literal meaning of the word. It can be translated as manners, habits, usage, way of life, but is not limited to any of these. What is customary in one place is not in another; national holidays, for example, most of them of a religious nature in Spain, are not observed in like manner in all parts of the country; they are subject to traditions peculiar to the region or even town. Loosely, then, so-called "costumbristic articles" portray a given place in a limited way, perhaps restricting the account to a single happening which may be analogous to happenings elsewhere, but is not the only way such things happen.

The first such article we find in this collection, "Historia de dos bofetones" (History of Two Slaps), is written in two parts. The first deals with how a mother handles the indiscretion of a girl in the seventeenth century. The second part is set in times contemporary to the author. In the first story the girl turns out all right, but in the second she goes from bad to worse. Other times, other customs, the author concludes. "El Lunes" (Monday) takes issue with the fact that although Martes (Tuesday) was named after Mars, the god of war, the really bad day is Monday, when all sorts of unpleasant things happen, mainly because most people are in a bad mood.

"El madrileño en la aldea" (The Madrid Dweller in a Village) depicts the adventures of Alfredo, a cultured young man born in Madrid, as he sets out to visit a small town for the first time in his life. Its counterpart is "El lugareño en Madrid" (The Villager in Madrid) with the city denizen's view of what such an experience must be for a peasant. Not unlike the preceding two is "Un viaje en galera" (A Trip on a Summer Stagecoach). In this instance Hartzenbusch wrote a chronicle of a journey he and a few friends had made in 1842, in his words for the benefit of future generations, since mankind is always eager to learn what its ancestors did.

"El jornalero" (The Wage Earner) observes the difference in customs in years past. Before, a man dressed according to his occupation, but not anymore. Workers change their attire and incorporate themselves into the group of employees of other, less menial jobs, to the point that they are confused with them in their appearance, even though in culture and manners they are not up to par. In a similar vein we find "Un entreacto" (Intermission), which compares the way in which the time elapsed between acts of a play was used centuries ago and in Hartzenbusch's time. The structure of the theater contributes to such difference also. Of a more personal nature is "Tropiezos de una escalera" (Stumbling on a Stairway), in which a homely young man gives an account of the difficulties he encounters going from his boardinghouse to visit a young woman in the building next door.

Two more articles are closer to the category of short stories, although the costumbristic aspect is present to some extent. "El mercader de la calle mayor" (A Main Street Merchant) depicts the everyday business district and ends with the author's philosophizing that the working class, if it is honest, can break through social barriers. "Querer de miedo" (To Love Out of Fear) is almost a short play. Pepita, sixteen years old, rejects Crispín Crispiniano Cabrejas, thirty years old, who has asked her in a letter to marry him. After some prodding from her mother, and the visit of two friends who deplore having turned down Crispín, the girl decides not to waste the opportunity to marry him.

CHAPTER 7

Hartzenbusch and His Editions of Spanish Classics

I   Fray Gabriel Téllez, Tirso de Molina

H ARTZENBUSCH published his edition of *Teatro escogido de Fray Gabriel Téllez, conocido con el nombre de El Maestro Tirso de Molina* (Selected Plays by Friar Gabriel Téllez, Known by the Name of Master Tirso de Molina) in twelve volumes, over the period of four years. Volume I, dated 1839, begins with a prologue in which Hartzenbusch states that the old *comedia* agonized in the arms of José de Cañizares. In the absence of theater of caliber, our author endeavored to revive the old plays, and began the task many times. He was not the first to have such an idea, although he criticizes a similar collection published by Vicente García de la Huerta the previous century. A second edition of that work would not fill the gap; he considered it of insufficient proportions, with great poets excluded and plays chosen erroneously or with poor taste. Hartzenbusch criticized two other collections for printing errors, poor quality paper, and excessive cuts due to censorship. Only one met with his approval: *Talía Española*, (Spanish Thalia), begun but not continued by Agustín Durán in 1834. It contained Tirso plays, so Hartzenbusch decided to publish the latter's best theater, some thirty-six works, with a critical examination of each one, as well as something about the author and his other plays. He hoped to avoid copying his spelling or his carelessness, to do away with errors, and eliminate bad teachings.

He would also divide the acts into scenes, which Tirso didn't do, to help keep better track of the action, to aid the reader, and to enhance the book. Notes would explain where the action takes place, and the meaning of words and phrases that seemed obscure. Somewhat paradoxically, he would not change a word when it was obviously a printing error and not Tirso's writing. Biographical material on Tirso would follow, taken from Agustín Durán's prologue to his *Talía*, in which he alludes to the old editions but does not mention his own. The plays follow, with an evaluation after each one.

Of *La villana de la Sagra* (The peasant girl from Sagra) Hartzenbusch says he chose it to start the collection since it contains the beauties and imperfections of the other dramas by Tirso, and so is sufficient to acquaint the reader with him. The editor finds that Tirso's people fall in love too quickly, that certain actions should not be done onstage, that at the end a scribe prevents a wedding, and asks why would Inés fall in love with Pedro if she is going to marry Feliciano. He comments that these mistakes and more are found in all of Tirso's plays and those of his contemporaries, but this one is ingenious. Hartzenbusch laments the lack of propriety of some of the thoughts expressed by the dramatist, and dislikes affected or ridiculous expressions in the mouth of his characters.

The first eleven volumes are treated the same way: they contain three plays each with very few notes, and varied commentary; he faults parts of each, sometimes the characters, often the choice of theme and words. Other such comments include his note in volume four that Tirso mentions the coming of the English to Cádiz in 1696[1] in the play *No hay peor sordo . . .* (There Is No Deafer Person . . .), and in volume seven, in *Averígüelo Vargas* (Let Vargas Find It Out), Hartzenbusch criticizes the girl protagonist's being almost a child[2] and a servant's bearing the name Tabaco (Tobacco), since this was not discovered until much later than 1441.[3] *Desde Toledo a Madrid* (From Toledo to Madrid), dated 1626, also in volume seven, is deemed to have been written more than six years after Tirso became a monk and was over fifty-five years of age.[4] Often Hartzenbusch comments that Tirso might well have dispensed with a character or with portions of acts. He also objects to excessive action as well as not enough of it, and points to anachronisms, ignoring his own. Taking some titles literally, he fails to see a secondary meaning, such as in *Amar por arte mayor* (To Love through Refined Art *or* To Love by Means of a High Poetic Form), a case wherein Hartzenbusch is clearly confused.[5]

Volume twelve, dated 1842, is supposed to contain an appendix to the series. It explains why, of the thirty-six plays Hartzenbusch intended to include, three had to be left out. The first is *El burlador de Sevilla* (The Deceiver of Seville), ostensibly because it was the first about don Juan Tenorio, and was both translated and staged excessively: by Molière, Corneille, Goldoni, Byron, Dumas, and many more. It is seen as bad, obscene, among the worst of Tirso's productions. In moral indignation, Hartzenbusch states that don Juan is a weak man, the plot is not original,[6] and Zamora's version is better.[7]

Tanto es lo de más como lo de menos (It is All the Same, More or Less), the second play omitted, was suppressed because it was still being performed in an updated version (not identified) as recently as 1839. Another reason was that it deals with a parable, and *El condenado por desconfiado* (Damned Because of Disbelief) was already printed in the series, although the parable is a different one. *Quien no cae no se levanta* (He Who Doesn't Fall Doesn't Get Up) was excluded because the second half of the second act was not worth much, literarily speaking; (up to that point it was deemed the best written but the most lascivious of Tirso). For these reasons, all three plays were abbreviated, following the action but "without linking words," he says.

As in the other eleven volumes, there are few footnotes, mostly brief, such as the observation that in his opinion a verse is missing. Page 209 provides excerpts of eleven other plays; page 350, notes to plays not included in the collection. One such play is *Los Amantes de Teruel* (The Lovers of Teruel), of which Hartzenbusch says it was imitated by Pérez de Montalbán and that he is indebted to both plays for the one he produced of the same title, discussed in chapter three of this book. He mentions a play by Andrés Rey de Artieda "earlier than the anonymous" work of the same title, another by Vicente Suárez, and three others on the same subject.

An account of the rest of Tirso's plays, or others attributed to him, follows. Of special interest is the note on *La Santa Juana* (Joan the Saint), concerning an incident when the first part of three was sent to the censor by Tirso. Hartzenbusch makes a comment (ultimately erroneous), reproducing the page in question in facsimile. If such an undertaking was possible in 1842 it means that many other things could have been proven that way.[8]

On page 389 there appears an index to the appendix, to which Hartzenbusch adds a note that in the biographical notes the first and second parts of Tirso's plays appear dated 1616, while *La villana de Vallecas* (The Peasant Girl from Vallecas) could not have been written until 1620. He avers that the oldest edition he has seen is dated 1626 (with the front cover bearing the date of a year later); he further says that even if it were a second printing, those who say 1616 may well have been mistaken.

II *More Tirso de Molina*

To the classic collection of *Biblioteca de Autores Españoles* (Library of Spanish Authors) Hartzenbusch contributed an edition of *Comedias escogidas de fray Gabriel Téllez (El maestro Tirso de Molina)* (Selected Plays by Friar Gabriel Téllez [Master Tirso de Molina]), published in Madrid in 1848, as volume five.[9] On page five of the prologue he thanks Agustín Durán, then director of the National Library, for materials put at his disposal, subsequently discussing actors' appropriation of plays, changing them as deemed suitable for performance, and otherwise altering the author's work. This situation was aggravated by printers, careless and unscrupulous in handling plays, from making mistakes to changing the name of the dramatist, helpless in the light of such mishandling of his work. He himself found manuscripts of Tirso plays which he judged unreliable, claiming they were copies made from printed works. Hartzenbusch is aware of the criticism he risks by touching the Spanish classics, but in his own eyes his is a work of restoration, destined for the *reading* public. To this end he introduces the divisions of acts into scenes whether Tirso used the word *acto* or *jornada*, and adds stage directions.

Page ten refers to the selection of plays included in this volume as being different from his previous edition (already commented on in this chapter), because of his feeling that the same selection should not be repeated. He adds three titles excluded before: *Cautela contra cautela* (Caution against Caution), *La ventura con el nombre* (Good Luck with the Name), and *Los Amantes de Teruel* (The Lovers of Teruel), which he says were very rare.[10] Beginning on page eleven are biographical and critical articles on Tirso by several learned critics. This section is followed by an annotated catalogue of Tirso's works, beginning with *Los cigarrales de Toledo* (The Country Houses of Toledo); next came the five parts in which the plays were printed. Hartzenbusch describes the editions consulted, stating he was unable to find the first. Of the thirty-six plays included in this edition, little information is given concerning some titles, while in other cases he quotes entire passages. Number five, *Los Amantes de Teruel*, is said to be copied exactly, leaving even the errors. He adds that Pérez de Montalbán based his play of the same title on this one, "which was probably also a reworking."[11]

By the fourth part, 1635, Hartzenbusch offers simply a line or two with an idea of what each of the twelve plays is about; he follows suit for part five, although some plays receive a greater share of lines than others. After this varied commentary upon what Hartzenbusch states are sixty-two plays, he recognizes a few more as works of Tirso, falling short of the four-hundred mark mentioned by his pseudonephew. Our editor counts seventy-eight, but without assigning a number mentions others, cautiously avoiding commitment as to whether he considers them genuine. Deploring his not possessing the manuscripts to ascertain which ones are the true work of Tirso, he seems to use this obvious handicap for the scholar as a stepping-stone for rendering his own version.

A long discussion of *El Rey Don Pedro en Madrid* (King Pedro in Madrid) follows, with the statement that aside from reworkings and defects, the phantom introduced in the play is worthy of Shakespeare. Hartzenbusch overlooks the fact that the Englishman's plays did not cross the sea until two hundred years after his death, while the Spanish classics were promptly translated and imitated shortly after they were written. Corneille and Molière are shining examples of this. Pages forty-one, forty-two, and forty-three mention manuscripts consulted in the library of the Duke of Osuna, thanks to the aid of the librarian and bibliophile Miguel de Salvá. Whatever advantage the opportunity represented is dubious; the three parts of *La Santa Juana* (Joan the Saint) consulted are quoted incorrectly[12] more than once, and subsequent research has shown that upon occasion Hartzenbusch did not consult manuscripts even when at his disposal.

Four appendixes at the end reproduce the third act of *Lo que hace un manto en Madrid* (What a Shawl Can Do in Madrid), excerpts of *El Rey Don Pedro en Madrid* (King Pedro in Madrid), observations on *La prudencia en la mujer* (Caution in Woman), and the Agustín Durán study on *El condenado por desconfiado* (Damned Because of Disbelief). All four appendixes are mentioned early on, but not cross-referenced.

III   *Hartzenbusch, Tirso de Molina, and the* Amantes de Teruel

Page twenty-one of the prologue quotes Mesonero Romanos to the effect that Pérez de Montalbán copied Tirso in *Los Amantes de Teruel;* on page twenty-eight Francisco Javier de Burgos is cited praising the versatility of Tirso and comparing excerpts of two plays, one the *Amantes*, but not hinting that it may not be Tirso's, as it is only attributed to him. Hartzenbusch repeats Mesonero Romanos, adding that it may be a remake. The text is followed exactly as found in the edition used, epitomizing how early books were printed. He has not even changed the punctuation (which he challenges constantly), and he finds fault with almost everything. What is interesting about the handling of this particular play is not his changing words and verses, or eliminating and adding things which may be justified in the eyes of the reader or scholar; here he is keeping quiet on aspects of the play that provided him with fodder to compose the one for which he is principally known.

There is not a word about the plot, the origin of the historic legend, the many works inspired by it, the studies made on the subject, the different ways in which each author handled the story. It seems Hartzenbusch intended not to credit Tirso with being his source, in spite of the brief mention in the 1839–1842 series on Tirso, in which he calls the play "anonymous." This is puzzling in a man who frequently pored over hundreds of books looking for information on a given item, no matter how small or irrelevant. Hartzenbusch made his own version of many plays by classic Spanish writers, dealing with historic events or people, national or foreign, ancient or contemporary; he placed notes of all kinds in his own plays, but in this instance he failed to say anything.

In his edition of Tirso plays, also in the Biblioteca de Autores Españoles, dated 1906, Emilio Cotarelo y Mori says of *Los Amantes de Teruel* that the play is not original either in theme or dramatic form, since Andrés Rey de Artieda[13] had touched it much earlier, and Montalbán copied him, too. In volume two of the same collection he repeats the statement in the annotated catalogue of Tirso's plays, and adds an account of other versions of the legend prior to Hartzenbusch's version.[14] Blanca de los Ríos, in her edition of Tirso's plays (Aguilar, Madrid, 1924), points out that Hartzenbusch's first edition of Tirso's plays, dated 1842, classified the *Amantes* as of doubtful attribution, but after Menéndez Pelayo said it could really be his, included it in the second edition.[15] Although Blanca de los Ríos's method is sometimes open to question, and she provides erroneous information, she seems convincing when identifying misstatements made by Hartzenbusch, so numerous and scattered that many scholars have copied them without question, and may never correct their misinformation.

Cayetano Alberto de la Barrera y Leirado, in his *Catálogo bibliográfico y biográfico del teatro antiguo español* (Bibliographic and

Biographic Catalogue of Old Spanish Theater), published in 1860, makes reference to catalogues, manuscripts, old editions, and rare books found in libraries to which scholars of the times had access, including the first play on the theme of the *Amantes*. If such information was available to others, it was also to Hartzenbusch, for various reasons. Page 324 states that Salvá gave Hartzenbusch an extensive bibliographical note on the play by Rey de Artieda for his edition of Tirso, and that it was printed, but I have not found it in any edition.[16]

IV   *Pedro Calderón de la Barca*

Bearing the dates 1848–1850, Hartzenbusch made his edition of *Comedias de don Pedro Calderón de la Barca* for the *Biblioteca de Autores Españoles* in four volumes. The first, number seven of the BAE collection, contains a lengthy prologue in praise of Calderón, but on page x the editor complains that he did not observe the dramatic unities except for that of action. On page xi Hartzenbusch makes a case for bringing out defects, grammatical errors, and faulty versification. He is bothered by the geographical jumps within a play, and situating a given city or country, mountain or river, in the wrong place, to say nothing of anachronisms and historic inaccuracies. In his opinion, if Calderón could not suit his plots to the stage he should have not touched mythology; however, there may be some who will pardon Calderón for his mythological plays since he was so good at the so-called "cape and sword" plays, he adds. He finds Calderón's language affected and unclear, but concludes that in his time he must have been understood, since he was so acclaimed. The four volumes he is preparing are all *comedias*, excluding *autos* and *entremeses*.[17] The *autos*, dramatic presentations of lesser duration than a regular-length play, are religious pieces dealing with the mystery of the Eucharist. The prologue is followed by different *aprobaciones* (permits) for several editions of Calderón's plays, together with forewords and other introductory material, and a total of twenty-five critical and biographical articles, bearing various dates. Page xli lists plays Calderón sent to the Duke of Veragua to Valencia in July of 1680.[18]

Hartzenbusch's handling of Calderón's theater is considerably different from that of the Tirso collection. He mentions looking for two plays which would bring the total to 120, but doesn't state the titles; the description of Calderón's previous editions, as well as other research material, is promised for volume four. Volumes two and three (ninth and twelfth of the series) are plays exclusively, without notes. Volume four, fourteenth of the series, contains a section concerning doubtful plays, in the eyes of Hartzenbusch. There is a list of editions consulted, but not having seen the first edition of the first part of Calderón's plays, he has used the one by Vera Tassis.

Hartzenbusch adds information about other editions he hasn't seen, but if he believes the date to be incorrect he says so, although how he can challenge something he hasn't seen is not explained. He goes on to say that he has corrected errors and noticed when a verse is missing, which he evidently has supplied. Unfortunately, he doesn't specify where he has done his restoration work. He offers a chronological catalogue of the plays, and another classifying them, plus notes to several plays with opinions by Alberto Lista, Manuel Bernardino García Suelto, Agustín Durán, and others. There is an appendix with an *entremés* and poems; then the index including all four volumes.

As with Tirso, there is ample information and commentary on some plays, yet not a word on others. Chronology is based on the date Calderón became a priest, since from that time on he wrote *autos sacramentales* (sacramental plays) and pieces for the king and his court, to be performed at the royal palace. This has its logic, although in the specific case of *La desdicha de la voz* (The Misfortune of the Voice) Hartzenbusch goes to great lengths to prove, via historic events, that the play dates from 1636, when the manuscript says clearly May 14, 1639.[19] An example of the few notes is the one found in *La niña de Gómez Arias* (The Girl of Gómez Arias), page 33. Don Diego has just rescued a girl from the hands of a black moor who was going to take her captive. Once the girl is safe, the gentleman says he was touched by her misfortune. Hartzenbusch notes in less than serious language that since the young woman hasn't told don Diego about her troubles this makes no sense.[20]

Comments in the chronological catalogue vary considerably. Exactly three lines of a double column are accorded to *La vida es sueño* (Life Is a Dream), one of the best-known plays of all times, much studied and translated. Six plays are given only a possible date, 1635, among them *El príncipe constante* (The Consistent Prince), also a well-known piece, and *El purgatorio de San Patricio* (The Purgatory of St. Patrick), which Calderón reworked from a play by the same title written by Juan Pérez de Montalbán in 1627. In the same situation we find *La niña de Gómez Arias* (The Girl of Gómez Arias), copied from an earlier play by Luis Vélez de Guevara. *Los*

cabellos de Absalón (The Hair of Absalom), based on a Tirso de
Molina play, is not described in any way.

In the last section, among other titles, are some five pages dedicated to *El alcalde de Zalamea* (The Mayor of Zalamea), one to *El
príncipe constante*, two each to *Amar después de la muerte* (To Love
after Death) and *A secreto agravio secreta venganza* (To a Secret
Offense a Secret Vengeance). One-half page is dedicated to *El médico
de su honra* (The Doctor of His Honor) and three-and-a-half columns
to *La vida es sueño*. This is followed by more notes on *El médico de su
honra*. The reader must seek this material, groping through the
entire book, since there are no notes or clues. The index covers only
the title given each section.

<h2 style="text-align:center">V   Juan Ruiz de Alarcón</h2>

Volume twenty of BAE, dated 1852, is dedicated to Juan Ruiz de
Alarcón y Mendoza. The fourth attempt to publish this collection on
the part of Hartzenbusch, it includes twenty-seven plays attributed
to Ruiz de Alarcón. A few titles are eliminated, leaving two that may
or may not be his. One is *Quién engaña más a quién* (Who Deceives
Whom the Most), which receives a commentary from Manuel Bernardino García Suelto. Other plays are discussed by other critics,
notably Alberto Lista. After establishing a relationship between the
two volumes published by the author, Hartzenbusch tries to arrange
the plays in chronological order. He has seen two copies of the second
volume without a license, so he assumes it must be a second edition,
and proceeds to establish his chronology, guiding himself by the king
or kings mentioned in some plays, and quoting scenes which provide
his base for placing a few *sueltas* (single, loose works) between the
lines of the list as it appeared in the first edition. For his corrections,
he uses the two volumes mentioned, and for the loose works any
collections that contained them, whether bound with Tirso de Molina
or different authors.

On page xv of the introductory material Hartzenbusch states that
practically nothing is known other than what can be gathered from
the derogatory writings or references of Góngora, Lope de Vega,
Quevedo, and others (more than a dozen) ridiculing Ruiz de Alarcón's
physical appearance.[21] The scant biographical material, despite dates
and footnotes, is based partly on conjecture, and therefore not
completely reliable. Notes and evaluation on the plays are placed ten
pages later, forcing the reader to go back and forth in order to com-

plete information that could have been included in a single section. Hartzenbusch praises the elegance of style, vocabulary, and thoughts displayed by Ruiz de Alarcón, whose plays have a very strong moralizing slant. The notes to the section just described also have their own footnotes, this time at the bottom of the page. The text of the plays follows. The paucity of notes suggests that if corrections were made, Hartzenbusch didn't specify. Commentaries and observations about the plays by many critics and writers form the last part of the volume. Rendered into Spanish are comments and thoughts of Corneille and Voltaire on the Ruiz de Alarcón plays that helped them to make their mark in the French theater.[22] These are followed by writings of Hartzenbusch's contemporary, Philarete Chasles. Presumably, the unsigned articles in this section are the work of the editor.

On page 547 the comment on *La prueba de las promesas* (The Proof of Promises) deals with the source story from *El Conde Lucanor* (Count Lucanor), one of the jewels of Spanish literature, containing numerous tales, morals, and wise examples. A newcomer to Spanish literature might take Hartzenbusch's information as accurate when he states, mistakenly, that its author wrote it in 1642.[23] The error comprises some three hundred years. Don Juan Manuel, the author, was a nephew of Alfonso X (The Wise); born in 1282, he died around 1348 or 1349. His *Conde Lucanor* dates from 1335, more than a decade before the *Decameron* (1348). While little is known even today about Ruiz de Alarcón, certain leads produce results. Professor Alva V. Ebersole has worked extensively on the subject, and I, as his wife, have been involved in it. To my satisfaction I found the record of enrollment of Juan Ruiz de Alarcón in the University of Salamanca, in the book containing such documents from 1597. It is dated October 25, 1600. It states that Ruiz de Alarcón transferred courses from Mexico, where he was born (Hartzenbusch mentions only that he came to Spain from Mexico and lived in Sevilla and Madrid).

VI *Lope Félix de Vega Carpio*

Volumes XXIV, XXXIV, XLI, and LII of the BAE contain the Hartzenbusch edition of selected plays by Lope de Vega. Any bibliographical note giving different numbers is erroneous, and the person giving it has copied it from a misinformed source, not having had the actual volumes in their hands. The extensive collection

known as BAE tends to cause great confusion to the scholar looking
for a specific item, due to exact but not overly explicit information
given as reference. Volume one of Lope de Vega in this instance is
twenty-four in the BAE series, but it doesn't follow that number two
of Lope is going to be twenty-five. For the sake of clarity, both
numbers should be given, especially when quoting volumes spora-
dically. The scholar knows what he is doing, but the reader does not
necessarily share with him this preliminary information. Even more
confusing is a reference to other volumes containing plays by the
same author, edited by someone else, as is the case of Lope and
Tirso. I have seen the third volume of Lope by Hartzenbusch listed as
number thirty-eight, actually another edition of Lope plays by
Cayetano Rosell. Aureliano Fernández Guerra offers this information,[24] which is repeated in numerous publications,[25] and Hartzenbusch's own son is of little help when he lists the fourth volume of that
particular set as forty-two.[26] For lack of an exact date we must rely on
Hartzenbusch's word that the task took him from 1853 to 1860. The
first volume, twenty-four of the series, contains in the prologue high
praise for Lope, stating that he wrote his first play at age eleven. He
doesn't give the title, so it is impossible to investigate further.
Hartzenbusch laments the absence of a good biography of Lope,
settling, not too happily, for the one left by Juan Pérez de
Montalbán,[27] supplemented by other source material. All this follows
a brief summary of the twenty-seven plays included in the volume.

The first play, *El verdadero amante* (The True Lover), is dedicated
to Lope's son. Hartzenbusch says it is not the first play by Lope but
the oldest known. Then he proceeds to demonstrate that it could be
the first, since his early plays were in four acts, and this one is in
three, but with the first act long enough to be a reworking of two acts
into one. For these reasons he transcribes the play without divisions
into scenes, as he does with the last. He has modernized the spelling
but prefers not to specify the corrections he had made in the text. Of
La Estrella de Sevilla (The Star of Seville) he says that some passages
were unclear or mutilated, or perhaps contained unfortunate additions, but again doesn't pinpoint what he has done. He promises
more information in the notes and expresses his intention of editing
three volumes of plays by Lope.

The texts, with very few notes, follow, and three appendixes: I, a
poem by Calderón de la Barca; II, debating whether or not a stanza is
Lope's or Ruiz de Alarcón's; III, an explanation of some of Calderón's
plays and an attempt to correct errors in his edition included in the

BAE, volumes seven, nine, twelve, and fourteen. While a new chronology is given, not all the errors are corrected.[28] The index closes the volume.

Number two, thirty-four of the series, begins with a preliminary note to *La Dorotea* by Francisco López de Aguilar. Twenty-eight plays follow, devoid of footnotes except for the notation of missing lines, and a correction followed by the index. The *advertencia* (notice) indicates that after the volume was printed he came upon the information that *La despreciada querida* (The Rejected Lover) is not Lope's, but was written by Juan de Villegas. Considering that the play occupies number fifteen in the book it is difficult to understand why it couldn't be taken out, avoiding confusion to generations to come at the expense of a bit of trouble for the printer. Erroneous dates Hartzenbusch assigned to plays by Ruiz de Alarcón and Tirso are rectified also.[29]

Volume three, forty-one of the series, contains thirty-two plays, without notes or corrections. The index promises an "advertencia," but there isn't any. Volume four, fifty-two of the series, has a prologue, wherein Hartzenbusch explains that he began the work on his edition of Lope de Vega's selected plays in 1853, and that it has taken him seven years to complete it. He regrets not having been able to consult other libraries because they are open only at the time he has to work in the National Library. This legitimate complaint is also a shelter for his mistakes, however, since he mentions other people working on editions of other writers, and a catalogue being compiled by Cayetano Alberto de la Barrera y Leirado.[30]

These preliminaries lead Hartzenbusch to retract and supposedly rectify errors in the last volume of Calderón, fourteen of the series, as well as in volume twenty, dedicated to Juan Ruiz de Alarcón. After a few pages on who wrote what, expressions and words that might be offensive in his time, but not when they were written, and the confusion that can result when not using the proper spelling, he adds more corrections. This time they are to set the record straight on things erroneous concerning his volumes published to date in the BAE series: Tirso de Molina (one), Ruiz de Alarcón (one), Calderón de la Barca (four), Lope de Vega (four). Only an Hispanist could possibly be interested in this, assuming he knew it was there. Here Hartzenbusch acknowledges, finally, that *La desdicha de la voz* (The Misfortune of the Voice), by Calderón, exists, in manuscript, in the library of the Duke of Osuna, bearing the date May 14, 1639.[31] Originally, Hartzenbusch established the date of the play in question in his own way; the second time he went further, stating that it was first performed in September 1636, some two and a half years before it was written.

Several prologues to Lope plays and lists of his works and those works of various authors follow, plus additional corrections to the prologue we are reading. *El mejor amigo el muerto* (The Best Friend Is the One Dead), act three of which he tried to prove belonged to Calderón, proves to be his indeed; he found the third act, although incomplete, in the library of the Duke of Osuna, bearing the first and last names of Calderón, and written in his own handwriting. Hartzenbusch could have left the pages dedicated to that play right where we find them, as with *La despreciada querida* (The Rejected Lover).[32]

The texts follow, with little or no informative material. At the end are more catalogues of Lope plays, with footnotes provided by Hartzenbusch to the plays discussed in the prologue, as well as *El mejor amigo el muerto,* and a long poem in praise of festivities in honor of the king, Felipe III. There is an adverse comment, also in verse form, on a piece by Juan Ruiz de Alarcón about the engagement of the Spanish princess María and the Prince of Wales, followed by an alphabetical list of the plays included in the Lope volumes and index. We count twenty-four in the last volume, but with the correction of one not being Lope's, and the addition of a title not by Lope it is impossible to ascertain by simply counting the titles in the index how many Lope plays are really published in this set; however, he has so many that give or take a few it makes little difference.

CHAPTER 8

Hartzenbusch and Cervantes

I *His Edition of the* Quijote

UNDER the auspices of don Manuel Rivadeneyra, a prominent bibliophile, editor, and printer, to whom the Biblioteca de Autores Españoles is indebted for its existence, as for his untiring promotion, editorship, and help, the complete works of Miguel de Cervantes saw the light.[1] The task was entrusted to Cayetano Rosell and Juan Eugenio Hartzenbusch. Printed in 1863, in twelve volumes, those numbered III, IV, V, and VI comprise the four dedicated to the *Quijote*, and are the work of our author, while others bear the name of Rosell. Dedicated to prince Sebastian Gabriel of Borbón and Braganza, this edition of the *Quijote* was printed in Argamasilla de Alba, in the house presumed to have been Cervantes's prison at one time. For that purpose, all necessary printing material was transported there. The work took from February 3 to May 9 of 1863, with the first few pages turned out by prince Sebastian Gabriel in person.

Let us examine the first volume, third of the series. The prologue, by Hartzenbusch (beginning on page VII), occupies twenty pages. While it is promised that notes on the prologue will be brief, the editor proceeds to waste paper and time with sometimes doubtful information. Hartzenbusch begins by saying that there was a Miguel christened October 9, 1547, in Santa María la Mayor of Alcalá de Henares, son of Rodrigo Cervantes and Leonor de Cortinas. He speculates that the child must have been born on September 29 of that year, feast of St. Michael. Another Miguel de Cervantes was baptized on November 9, 1558, eleven years later, in Alcázar de San Juan, son of Blas Cervantes Saavedra and Catalina López. Hartzenbusch concludes that one of the two is the author of the *Quijote*.[2] Explaining that even though "Saavedra" is not consigned to the first Miguel de Cervantes, he observes that other data about his writings, the wound in his left hand, and his long captivity coincide. After a list of works of Cervantes and their dates he comes to the place where this particular edition was printed: Argamasilla de Alba. Hartzenbusch conjectures that it must be the place whose name Cervantes didn't want to remember, as stated in the opening lines of the *Quijote*, because due to an infraction of local laws he was imprisoned in the house of a man named Medrano, whose cave served as jail in the absence of one in the town.

Hartzenbusch attributes to certain derogatory remarks in the prologue of the *Quijote* the irate response of an unidentified man from Tarragona, who published in 1614 a second part to the *Quijote*, when Cervantes had completed fifty-eight of its seventy chapters. Sick, and sixty-seven, he hurriedly finished his masterpiece. Allegedly a certain Rodrigo Pacheco was responsible for whatever unpleasantness Cervantes experienced in Argamasilla. After seeing a painting of don Rodrigo and a young lady praying in the church of Argamasilla, (with a legend stating that Our Lady appeared to that gentleman after he prayed to her to relieve him of an illness that left his brain cold), Cervantes took him as his model for don Quijote. Don Rodrigo's house is rubble now, Hartzenbusch says, but not the prison in the house of Medrano, or the fantasy Cervantes created in his masterwork. The house, acquired by prince Sebastian Gabriel, was used for the printing of this particular edition of the *Quijote* as an artistic, historic, and soulful touch.

Hartzenbusch decided to consult the first edition to compose his own. Reviewing assorted names of editors, printers, and dates, he concludes that the first of the three "primitive" editions is the worst. He bases his assertion on lapses of memory by the author or printer. As for the second part of the novel, not only does he find errors, but he criticizes Cervantes for not correcting the proofs.[3] According to our editor, if Cervantes didn't object to glaring errors, they were printed. He maintains that Cervantes didn't even read his first draft of the *Quijote*, or the first edition and, if a man of fifty-seven tends to be forgetful, Cervantes was so even twenty years before, when he wrote the *Galatea*. Hartzenbusch blames on Cervantes' economic needs the conjectures that Cervantes composed his episodes one at a time, and tried to link them in a whole that the printer and other assorted people working on it filled with mistakes, a situation aggravated by Cervantes's handwriting. To prove this he points out that in a document he found in Simancas, Cervantes even forgot one *a* in Saavedra, and in other words he had *o* instead of *a*, and that there is an *r* missing here and there. We are not provided with a facsimile to judge his reading.[4]

Hartzenbusch commends editions by several Spanish scholars and proceeds to make his own. He frustrates the investigator when (on page xx) he states that his variants are not marked by footnotes because they distract the reader, and also that after the text was printed he decided that some of his observations were not good, but leaves the whole thing unexplained.

Hartzenbusch claims that the two consecutive years in which Cervantes places the action of the adventures of don Quijote are arbitrary and full of anachronisms, so he will set the record straight. He rejects the years 1604–1605 Vicente de los Ríos established when he prepared his own monumental edition of the *Quijote* for the Royal Spanish Academy. In the same paragraph he defends the original, spontaneous work of Cervantes as something nobody has a right to touch, but since the original is not available he is going to do what he pleases. A long panegyric of Cervantes's life, linking it with the various characters and situations depicted in the novel, ends the prologue, with verses to Cervantes by his own *Don Quijote*, pertaining to the end of an unidentified play written in prose.

Pages xxix to xxxii contain a diary for the better understanding of the travels and adventures of don Quijote. According to Hartzenbusch the first part begins in 1589 and the second in 1614. His chronology, specific as to actual dates and days of the week of a given year, such as Friday, July 28, 1589, attempts to show discrepancies in days and months, as if all events were historic and subject to exact time, not to imagination and fable. In three pages of small print and full of dates, Hartzenbusch attempts to be more specific than is possible in trying to ascertain the exact time of travels and comings and goings of the hero. This takes us back to the editor's starting point: some things can't be established beyond the shadow of a doubt. Losing sleep over dates may mean depriving oneself of the pleasure of reading the book.

II *The Notes to the* Quijote

After many days' work on the first volume of the first part, I found the task absurdly difficult due to the stumbling blocks placed in the way of the scholar by Hartzenbusch. Given the number of notes it would be futile to attempt a complete translation and commentary on each one of them, since that is peripheral to the purpose of this book, and lest I leave out everything else. Hispanists who so desire can better judge Hartzenbusch's notes by poring over the collection discussed here, described and included in the bibliography. There is also a facsimile of the first edition of the *Quijote*, ultimately used by Hartzenbusch for his own work, which Alfaguara, The Hispanic Society of America, and *Papeles de Son Armadans* (Palma de Mallorca) issued jointly in 1968. This two-volume set (limited to a printing of 750 copies, available by subscription) can be found in the library of several universities in the United States.

The text is rendered with changes of words and punctuation, and additions that are explained in some instances and not in others. His slant is more grammatical than logical, although in many situations the changes are not strictly necessary. The lack of specific numbers to the notes in the proper place complicates checking them. At the end of the first volume are 280 notes of varying lengths and relevancy. Having to go back to the text to hunt for each one of them is a time-consuming and unrewarding task. While this is done or undertaken the narrative thread is lost. Hartzenbusch directs the reader's attention to the middle of a page, or so many lines counting from the end of a given paragraph. Such references to lines in terms of approximate place in the text are a threat to the reader's eyesight and sanity. These are a few examples: note 169, page 148, "At more than half"; note 195, page 177, "After the half"; note 201, page 183, "Beginning of the paragraph before the next to the last"; note 227, page 210, "Lines next to the last and last of the first paragraph of chapter XXIII"; note 4, page 264, "Page viii, lines three and four, counting from the last of the middle paragraph;" note 39, page 281, "Page L lines before next to the last, next to the last and last". For the sake of clarity, then, notes will be identified only by number.

III   *Volume I*

The first volume, third of the series, has the first note on pages 261–62. It refers to the front page of the first edition and has a description of the book. Hartzenbusch claims that there are two pages, numbered 7 and 182, respectively, without 8 and 183. According to my facsimile this is not true. It is equally erroneous that there are two 311s and no 310, and pages 25 and 27 are so numbered, not 225 and 227 as he claims.

On page xxxix of the prologue Hartzenbusch respects the reading of the facsimile *oillo o leelle,* modern *oirlo o leerle,* (listen to or reading it) but changes *agora* to *ahora* (now) and in general modernizes spelling as he pleases. He also disregards paragraph division, commas, periods, question marks, and exclamation points, and adds or eliminates parentheses at will, without saying a word about such changes. Even when Cervantes proceeds to delight the reader with all the invented poems in praise of the book, the characters, or the author, as was customary at the time, Hartzenbusch indents verses and separates them into sets without following Cervantes. Similarly treating the punctuation or lack of it, he gets into hot water trying to analyze his own reading of the passage, as seen in several notes, some of which follow.

Note 4: "With the surname of Saavedra, which the one from Alcalá does not have." As to the last name Saavedra, the editor observes that it was customary in Spain in ages past to take the surname from somebody in the family, even to the exception of that of the father or the mother; hence Cervantes took Saavedra, as his great-grand-mother Juana de Avellaneda did, who took her mother's surname instead of her father's, Juan Arias de Saavedra. If this is so, why introduce the second Cervantes? If Hartzenbusch was previously in doubt, as stated in pages vii and viii of the prologue, it seems odd that he is suddenly so sure of who Cervantes's ancestors were.

Note 16: "See toward the middle, page 22 of volume IV of this edition. Go back to page 130 of this first volume, next-to-the-last paragraph" (refers to page xxiii). This simple explanation is intended to prove something about the verb *regoldar* (to burp). However, there is no such reference on page xxiii of the first volume, or on page 130. Page 22 of the fourth volume, chapter XLIII, contains a dialogue between don Quijote and Sancho about the impropriety of the word *regoldar,* and how it should be said, that is, *eructar.* A patient search revealed that the passage Hartzenbusch refers to is found on page xxi, not xxiii, of the first volume, an error he did not correct, so that turning to page 130 does not help at all. The reference on page xxi points out that *regoldar* was considered a coarse word, and Hartzen-busch contrasts this with the use of other words that we find offensive today which were freely used then. Specifically, a character calls his maid *puta* (whore).

Note 17. This note from the director of the Madrid observatory concerns the phases of the moon during July 1589, supposing that a particular Friday, the twenty-eighth, was the day Cervantes had in mind if he followed the natural phenomena.

Note 21. By eliminating, Hartzenbusch has changed *pues*, meaning "besides," to *pues*, meaning "as long as." Cervantes's version is perfectly understood and not incorrect. Hartzenbusch also placed parentheses where there are none in the text, or none are necessary.

Note 24. Cervantes excuses the lack of quotations because he doesn't have anything to put in as marginal notes, or at the end, and anyway he wouldn't know what authors to quote. To me this means he is not going to bother with that but use what comes to mind as relevant to the story. To Hartzenbusch this means that Cervantes probably had no books, a sure sign of poverty.

Note 28: "In the valley of Terebinto." Hartzenbusch states that Cervantes must have called that note *grand* because some writer, ignorant of the fact that *terebinto* is a kind of tree, thought it to be the name of a place. In the Bible, in the first book of Samuel (in some versions called the first book of Kings), number seventeen, it is stated that Saul and the children of Israel came to the valley of *Terebinto* to fight the Philistines. As Hartzenbusch makes no mention of this, perhaps he didn't find it in the Bible.[5]

Notes 35 and 37. In these two notes Hartzenbusch implies that certain remarks directed at Sancho Panza indicate there was more than one such character, based on words that he interprets in a strict sense, leaving no room for the versatility of the word in question or the invective and festive tone of Cervantes. When the poet writes to Sancho and the horse Rocinante, or in their behalf, it may be unclear due to lack of punctuation, as seen in the facsimile. Hartzenbusch and others added their own, and in trying to interpret the passage, made it more baffling. This is really amusing in note thirty-eight:

> Note 38. "Que esto saqué a Lazari—
> Cuando, para hurtar el vi—
> Al ciego, le *vi* la pa—."

The facsimile has no punctuation and says *di* (I gave) instead of *vi* (I saw). The passage refers to the horse and how he learned to look after himself from Lazarillo de Tormes, who stole wine from his blind master with a straw. Hartzenbusch states that this correction, from the horse giving the straw to the boy, to seeing it and imitating his example, is to the credit of Manuel Bretón de los Herreros.

Now, if Rocinante was (in fact) able to speak, observe Lazarillo, learn to steal from him, and write about it in verse, why couldn't he give the boy the straw to seep the wine? It is interesting that these two gentlemen, Bretón and Hartzenbusch, pick on this perfectly logical point but do not notice the fantasy of Rocinante being a namesake, or the real great-grandson of Babieca, the horse of the Cid. Strictly speaking, there is no record of how long Babieca lived, or of his descendency, if any. The Cid died in 1099, and assuming his horse survived him a few years (data I shall carefully note next time I visit San Pedro Cardeña, where both, master and horse, are buried, along with other members of the household), just how long does a horse live? From 1099 to 1589, which Hartzenbusch claims is the first outing of don Quijote, is 490 years.[6]

Note 234. Hartzenbusch corrected the word *naked* to read *half* naked. "He wasn't really completely naked, since he wore breeches and doublet." If Hartzenbusch had read the passage carefully, he would have noticed that the young man *seemed* naked to don Quijote, who saw him from a distance.[7]

Note 255. For no reason the editor changes the word *señor*, referring to Amadís de Gaula as unsurpassed in his feats, to "fénix" (phoenix).

Note 260. Hartzenbusch arbitrarily places the passage of the missing donkey where he thinks Cervantes might have put it. The facsimile edition has the missing passage on page 96 of the second edition, which corresponds to chapter XXIII, folio 108 of the facsimile.

Note 267: "On leaves of *certain* trees. Ordinary text: On tree leaves. Cervantes must have made clear that the letter to Dulcinea couldn't be written on the leaves they had around." Hartzenbusch doesn't give Cervantes or don Quijote credit for any common sense. Besides, the text refers to the way letters were written in antiquity, on tree leaves or wax tablets. Who would undertake to write on mimosa or weeping-willow leaves?

Note 274. "There are several instances in which *por* was printed instead of *para* in our book. Perhaps Cervantes wrote his preposition in a confusing abreviation".

It could be that he meant "due to how much I love Dulcinea" (por) and not "for what I want Dulcinea for" (para) which put out of context is not a nice thing to say.

Note 279: " 'On August 30' is the way the date should read,

according to our diary, which we do not defend. Our liberty is excused by the fact that the first and second editions by Cuesta have August 22, and the third reads the 27th. Being both doubtful dates, we have selected another. The numbers must not have been very clear if they were so differently read, leaving the doubt as to whether even the second time they were well interpreted."

IV   Volume II

The second volume of this edition, fourth of the series, also printed in Argamasilla de Alba, begins with chapter XXVI of the first part of the *Quijote*, ending with chapter LII, the last. Pages 356 to 412 contain three hundred notes pertaining to those chapters, followed by the index. Hartzenbusch blames Cervantes for not supervising personally the printing, or letting the variations introduced by other people stand. In several notes Hartzenbusch states what he thinks are contradictions, missing pages or passages and superfluous ones, and amends the text to his liking. As many notes are picayune or a matter of spelling, a few examples will suffice.

Note 4 registers an objection as to how don Quijote improvised a rosary while doing penance in Sierra Morena. He ties knots on a strip torn from the bottom part of his shirt, and offers one million "Hail Marys." Hartzenbusch consulted the second edition by Cuesta, and taking part of what somebody emended there, and a little of the first edition, made up his own version, which reads that don Quijote made a rosary of galls from a cork tree, and the prayers were one thousand.

Note 5: "To sorrowful and *timid* Eco. The other editions: 'To sorrowful and humid Eco.' Referring to imitator Eco, an earth nymph, it seems unnatural that Cervantes would apply the adjective *humid,* more suitable to water nymphs: *timid* would suit her better, since echo always speaks from afar." In volume four, second appendix, number four, we find: "Volume II, page 4, close to the end. (See the note to this, page 388 of said volume. In the first volume of *Works of Lope* [*Obras sueltas*] one reads, on page 198: 'Echo, in other times a nymph, and for treason/ to June, her mistress,/ . . . She changed her to voice, that answers timidly/ from her hollow hiding place.' " Aside from his missing the metaphor, the page to which Hartzenbusch refers the reader is not 388 as stated, but 358. [8]

Note 122. This note takes more than half a page and concerns a verb tense. It merits little further, since the first time around the editor concluded that maybe changing the punctuation the passage could be left as it read in the primitive text, anyway.

Note 260. Hartzenbusch takes issue with the use of the word *señor* (gentleman, master) instead of *héroe* (hero), and although he hasn't found the latter in any of the old editions of the *Quijote* he puts it in his own of 1863.

V *Volume III*

The third volume, fifth of the series, begins with the second part of the *Quijote* and goes through chapter XL. Of similar size to the preceding ones, it contains 226 notes. In note 3, Hartzenbusch speculates on whether or not Cervantes was involved in Lepanto or wishes he had been. This is clearly rendered by Cervantes. If Hartzenbusch had read the passage well he would have seen that it begins by stating that if he could he would again take part in the battle at Lepanto. Hartzenbusch seems to realize his error when he concludes Cervantes could not have meant that, so it must be a printer's error.

Note 33. Hartzenbusch objects to Sancho's expression, mixing cabbages with baskets (*berzas con capachos*), referring to the disparaging things said by Cide Hamete. Being items of different nature, the editor contends they cannot be confused with one another, as would be the case with two types of cabbages or baskets. He goes on to explain the meaning of the word *capacho* and the varieties of it, but ends up saying that in spite of everything Covarrubias lists Sancho's words as a proverb.

With that information I pored through Covarrubias's dictionary unsuccessfully. At the end of volume four, appendix two, note eight, however, Hartzenbusch retracts his words by saying that it should read as in the first edition, not as he printed it. The popular saying, he says, is in Covarrubias, under *herreñal*, page 468. This time I found it in my modern edition, page 684, but only because I remembered this particular note, not referred to by number in the appendix. As it states only that it is "volume III, page 27, at the end" one has to look for the passage, turn to the notes and hunt for those that might be near that page.

Note 143. Hartzenbusch says: "Cabeza y *manos*" (Head and hands). "First edition: 'Cabeza y cabellos', (Head and hair). The issue here is to scratch, for which hands are necessary; the word is not in the other editions, and it must not be the author's fault." If we follow Hartzenbusch's logic, Adam, to whom the passage refers, scratched his bald head with his hands.[9]

VI   *Volume IV*

The fourth volume, sixth of the series, contains chapters XLI to LXXIV, last of the second part of the *Quijote*. The notes, in the same vein as those in the preceding volumes, number 206. A single example will suffice.

Note 112. This curious note concerns the expression "Santiago y cierra España," used in ancient times by Spanish armies. The clear invocation to St. James, the apostle, followed by an enigmatic "and close ranks, Spain" is translated literally, not meaningfully. Through etymology and the normal usage which causes attrition, it comes to mean "save, or guard Spain." Hartzenbusch questions the antiquity of such expression in view of the fact that he hasn't found it in the *Poema del Cid*, or the *Navas* (1212) and other battles. Hartzenbusch doesn't find it plausible that the people who converted *Sancte Jacobe* to *Santiago* couldn't find a better word for "save" and left "cierra" (close) when it meant "fight, attack." Our editor once again considers Spain the whole territory it now occupies regardless of national unity or lack of it. "Cierra España" would have been an anachronism in times of El Cid.

VII   *Appendixes to Volume IV*

The notes to volume four are followed by two appendixes. The first, pages 345 to 352, contains fragments of observations Hartzenbusch published in 1845 in the Madrid newspaper *El Laberinto* (The Labyrinth) on the comments to *Don Quijote* by Diego Clemencín. The second appendix, pages 353 to 362, contains twenty emendations to supplement notes to the four volumes. As might be expected, Hartzenbusch did not refer to his correction in the second appendix by number, only by page and lines up or down; therefore the scholar has to turn back to his text, and thence to the notes, and hunt for some that may be near that particular page. For example, note 8 retracts what the editor said in note 33 to the third volume (see text).

Hartzenbusch appended to the *Quijote* 1,032 notes, many super-fluous, a defect other books also have. Some of his observations are unnerving, while others are very educational and might send the curious reader to the *Covarrubias,* a delightful reference book in many instances, or otherwise to pursue a given item. His edition of the *Quijote* has notes which are doubtful and in no way reflect all the changes Hartzenbusch made in the text. His not listing notes by number as they occur, and his not confessing to changes, make his version of *Don Quijote* an unreliable one.

VIII *Hartzenbusch and His 1633 Notes to the* Quijote

Not satisfied with his work on the *Quijote* for Rivadeneyra, Hartzenbusch revised it, and eleven years later, in 1874, he gave the world another book on the subject. The complete title reads *"Las 1633 notas puestas por el excmo. e ilmo. Sr. D. Juan Eugenio Hartzenbusch a la primera edición de el Ingenioso Hidalgo reproducida por D. Francisco López Fabra con la fototipia.* Barcelona, Ramírez, 1874" (The 1633 Notes Put by the Excellent and Illustrious Mr. Juan Eugenio Hartzenbusch to the First Edition of the *Ingenious Gentleman,* Reproduced by Francisco López Fabra with Phototype. Barcelona, Ramírez, 1874).

The book begins with a foreword by Hartzenbusch concerning editions of the *Quijote* and continues with the notes. Unlike the previous annotated edition, which contains the text of the novel, this one is made up purely of notes, some new, some repeated, others enlarged, with an attempt at correction, and even footnotes to the notes.[10] Beginning with the front page of the first three editions, the notes go through the permits, dedications, prologues, and notes to anything on the text.[11] The first part of the *Quijote* is thus annotated in 109 pages, with 1,011 notes. Before the second part there is a notice about additions that should be made in certain notes, others left out involuntarily, or what might be added.[12]

The second part covers notes 1,012 to 1,633, to page 185. Pages 187 to 192 are taken up by the conclusion. With his habitual humility, the editor recommends that more editions and corrections to the *Quijote* be made, and to the entire production of Miguel de Cervantes. After the conclusion there is an article on Cervantes and Lope de Vega in 1605 that Hartzenbusch published in 1862, and from which he deleted certain parts. According to him, if Cervantes conceived his idea of don Quijote based upon the person of Lope de Vega, the adjective "ingenioso" (ingenious) was certainly most appropriate.

The Hispanist can refer to these 1,600-odd notes and compare them to the more than a thousand published in 1863, if he is so inclined. A few examples of Hartzenbusch's laborious research will suffice for the less specialized. Many notes consist of a word substitution, but since it is not always given in context it is impossible to judge. When to the first edition, it is hard to find a justification for the constant references not only to the second and third by the same printer, Cuesta, but to two made in Brussels, in 1607 and 1611 respectively, between which oftentimes there is no distinction made. It is evident that many objections raised by Hartzenbusch are directed to Cervantes's way of writing, his vocabulary, or an intended pun, usually missed by our editor, but he keeps blaming the printer as a safeguard.

With the juggling of editions the folio number does not necessarily correspond to that of the facsimile first edition, if we take into consideration that the three main such printings are the first by Cuesta, Hartzenbusch's own text, with the resulting difference in page numbering due to his additions, and the López Fabra text, which is not included with the notes. In the prologue to the 1,633 notes it is mentioned that they are found at the end of each volume, but we are neither told how many there are nor given their numbering; such information does not accompany any of the notes, and the only division is that of the two parts of the *Quijote*.

There seems to be no specific criteria followed in these annotations; it is evident that Hartzenbusch did not consult the first set of notes in most cases. He claims to have consulted several editions, and some notes are common sense and others are really observations on his part. A comparison of the 1863 four-volume edition and the 1874 set of notes shows that they are more numerous in the latter after the first fifty, as we find note 54 corresponds to number 61 of the second set; 61 to 82, 82 to 105, 98 to 143, 130 to 196, 163 to 256, 171 to 281, 221 to 368, and 251 to 424. Some notes coincide slightly, but there is a great deal of contrast in the handling.

IX *The Notes*

Note 17: "Quizá escribió Cervantes *Valle de Terebinto,* aludiendo al error de alguno, que había usado este nombre de localidad, ignorando que terebinto es árbol, y que el mencionado Valle se ha llamado siempre no de Terebinto, sino del Terebinto". This is quite a change from the cutting comment in earlier notes to the *Quijote,* where not one mention is found as to the valley even being named in the Bible. He remains ignorant of this fact, but finds a way to flaunt his erudition by mentioning a work not well known and making conjectures he himself almost rejects.

Note 37. Again what Hartzenbusch now maintains is diametrically opposed to what he said the first time, when he severely criticized this passage about Rocinante giving Lazarillo a straw. [13]

Note 388. The same observation as the first time is made, altering the text, but now Hartzenbusch quotes from Covarrubias to prove that wearing underwear is to be half naked. [14]

Note 457. "Dated. . .August 22. This is the same as in the second Madrid edition; the third reads August 27." This time only the dates are given as shown in the three early versions, without challenge or comment.

Note 468. The editor transcribes the passage as in the facsimile, observing that Cuesta in his two editions, and all others that follow, read: "The most he did was to pray, and so will I. And served him as a rosary galls from a cork tree he strung together, making ten." "A convenient correction, whoever made it, because a rosary made of a dirty rag sounds bad, even if it is the work of a madman."

Note 470. In this instance the observation made is the same, without reference to Lope. Despite Hartzenbusch's failure to capture it, the implication is very clear: Eco's *humidity* is not her own, but an allusion to her hopeless love for Narcissus, infatuated with his own image to the point that he worshiped his beauty reflected in the water. Eco wasted away until only her voice was left. [15]

Note 919. In keeping with his objections to the word *señor* raised in the 1863 edition, volume I note 255, and volume II note 260, Hartzenbusch's theory is that *señor* instead of *héroe*, that is, *gentleman* instead of *hero,* does not fit the main character. However, he contradicts himself somewhat when he brings about the explanation of *heroic* to mean *mayor o señor* (*highest* or *master*) in two different works, seeing only that they try to explain the meaning of *hero;* therefore he chooses this word instead of what Cervantes wrote.

Note 1012. This first note to the *Second Part* of the *Quijote* takes issue with the title. The objection is to calling the hero *caballero* (knight) instead of *hidalgo* (a variation of gentleman).

Note 1017. Hartzenbusch, disregarding the surname Avellaneda, so close to Cervantes's relatives, speculates whether the author of the spurious second part of the *Quijote* was not a friar, Luis de Aliaga, fond of the theater and offended by the mock name given him, Sancho Panza, as whoever wrote the second part calls the novel a farce and a comedy.

Note 1020. Hartzenbusch quotes two lines of the statement made by Cervantes about how he would rather have been at Lepanto than safe and sound now. Without going back to his earlier note of 1863, he offers the usual suspicion of the printer changing words, and endeavors to impose his own reading of the passage. The quotation from the first edition is incomplete, so this note is superfluous.[16]

Note 1458. "About the expression 'Santiago y cierra España.' 'Is Spain by chance open, so it is necessary to close it? Or what ceremony is this?' A question of Sancho's, to which his master does not answer. Further on Sancho calls him *son of a bitch,* and good don Quijote is not offended. Also, master and servant dine twice on the same day: there is, in a word, a great deal of disorder in this chapter. As in the next chapter Cervantes speaks of the *Quijote* by Avellaneda, perhaps the defects are due to Cervantes being at this point in his work, when there came to his hands the book in which. . .he was insulted and which pretended to rob the utility of his manuscript; and the poor old man, sixty-seven already, was upset, shaken, disturbed in terms of not being able to pay the necessary attention to what he was writing."

The notes exceed the numbers indicated, since Hartzenbusch annotated his own notes and made additions; the count, therefore, is not accurate. If Hartzenbusch had been less hasty, he would have saved everybody the trouble of being wrong. Mine is not the first word of caution regarding taking Hartzenbusch as the supreme authority, but because of this book I am in a better position to point this out in many of his works, not simply a single play or article. When Hartzenbusch is correct he proves his skill and knowledge, but at other times, he simply can't be trusted.

X *Conclusion*

Unquestionably Hartzenbusch had a lyric vein, sensitivity, and enough artistic spirit to work in a versatile manner. This gift, however, seems to have been counterbalanced by what is generally termed as a Germanic knack for detail, investigation, polishing, and research of fine points, which he used with varying degrees of fairness. Also the temptation he evidently felt to experiment with someone else's life as found in history books, and to rework plays and themes as written by other people, together with his inability to separate the scholar from the artist, weighs very heavily. His thirst for knowledge led him to dabble in translations to which he added his own ideas, seemingly walking the thin line between imitation and plagiarism. In the case of the fables he compiled, it was most certainly a constructive contribution; in the area of some dramatic works there is ample room for doubt. The same is true when he chose to bring into his theater undesirable traits or imaginary, ill-conceived passions which he somehow felt would enhance the play.

Granted that the best way to preserve dramatic works is the written form, a mere reading of them doesn't fulfill the main function of theater. It must come to life onstage. Footnotes are of no value to an audience which cannot read them. If a word can't be made clear in context it should not be used. If historical facts are deliberately bent, the audience must be informed from the stage, by an actor reciting his role. Any other means borders on failure for the playwright, whose duty is to convey his plot to the audience and not to write it down for scholars. I have stated my position on this matter elsewhere and in Spanish, so I feel justified in making such a comparison in English: if a piece of music is to be dissected there can be no music left if only the form is studied, to see if it conforms to rules invented after the art became recognized as such, and that alone can't be the last word; music has to be performed or heard to be appreciated. There is also a difference between a recording and a live performance; the former may be perfect since it is possible to correct mistakes; the latter has only one chance, but it has the attraction of the real thing, which cannot be equaled. The same principle can be applied to a dramatic work.

Throughout his work there are clear signs of Hartzenbusch's being a believer mixed with complaints of the little reward that doing good things brings, but he is not an exception in the way he treats the fate of many characters that are mentioned in passing and soon forgotten. An injustice done a main character is decried by the author, but peripheral victims of murder, jilted lovers, and the like are not taken into consideration when the guilty person attains power, marries to his advantage, or is forgiven by authorities against whom he hasn't transgressed in the first place. Hartzenbusch had a twisted sense of mockery when he used derogatory, cacophonous, or downright ugly names for his characters, but he was very careful not to do so when they were foreign. Such ridicule, in questionable taste, was partial to his Spanish heritage, from which, by the way, he obtained any refinement or artistry in his intellect, since his father is described in most of the biographical material as a poor carpenter, not interestsd in much of anything. However, Hartzenbusch seems to have been in constant quest for his German heritage by learning the language, reading extensively, translating, imitating, and in general emulating German theater and fables, as well as working untiringly at discovering vestiges of Germanism within his being.

Certain erroneous information Hartzenbusch published as fact has been faithfully copied by many scholars. Even in cases where he later found new items or evidence and had it printed as a correcting note, the initial damage was done. There is no guarantee that the reader will see the new discovery. Hartzenbusch occasionally adds a note beginning with a statement such as "after the prologue was printed" or "after the book was printed" and then proceeds to set the record straight. Who can believe such a thing when the correction is included, printed, and bound in the same volume, and not even on a separate sheet or the last page? Such patchwork constitutes a disservice to readers and scholars. Misleading or withheld information in the specific case of *Los Amantes de Teruel* suggests that Hartzenbusch wanted to keep to himself the sources used for his own version of the play based on the historic legend. Despite his limitations, however, his place in history is not to be denied him. While exhibiting much that is exemplary, Hartzenbusch is equally representative of the typical scholarly vices of his day. Good, bad, and indifferent, his work belongs to his century, and there—attacked on one hand, overrated on the other—his position seems secure.

Notes and References

Preface

1. Andrés Rey de Artieda, *Los Amantes*. Tirso de Molina, *Los Amantes de Teruel*. Edición e introducción de Carmen Iranzo. Madrid, 1971.

Chapter One

1. Antonio Peña y *Goñi*. La ópera española y la música dramática en España en el siglo XIX. Madrid, 1881.
2. As this is discussed at length in a forthcoming TWAS volume, *Antonio Garcia Gutierrez,* I will not expand on this point.
3. *"Bibliografía de Hartzenbusch* (Excmo. Sr. D. Juan Eugenio) formada por su hijo D. Eugenio Hartzenbusch, del cuerpo facultativo de Archiveros, Bibliotecarios y Anticuarios. Tirada de 500 ejemplares. Madrid. Establ. tipográfico "sucesores de Rivadeneyra" Impresores de la Real Casa. Madrid, 1900." "Bibliography of Hartzenbusch (Distinguished Mr. Juan Eugenio) by his son Eugenio Hartzenbusch, of the corps of Archivists, Librarians and Antique dealers. A 500-copy edition. Madrid, Printing shop of the heirs of Rivadeneyra, printers of the Royal House. Madrid, 1900."

Chapter Two

1. El no haber mencionado Lope esta comedia en ninguna de las dos ediciones (1604 y 1618) de *El peregrino en su patria* y el no haberla incluido en ninguna de las Partes de sus comedias, que preparó antes de morir, motivó que el hispanista Foulché-Delbosc asegurara tan terne—en la *Revue Hispanique,* tomo XLVIII—que *La Estrella de Sevilla* no era de Lope. ¡Buenojo clínico! El señor Foulché-Delbosc, discreto investigador de nuestra historia literaria, desbarró siempre que quiso suponer por su cuenta. Lo peor del caso es que numerosos críticos españoles, auténticos papanatas cuando se trata de admirar lo extranjero, han dado como válida una opinión tan catastrófica" (p. 539).
2. Professor de Armas's analysis awaits publication in the Scottish journal *Forum for Modern Language Studies.*
3. The statement that a priest pleads for his son, in Catholic territory, is obviously a device to startle the audience, since Roman Catholic priests cannot marry and have legitimate progeny.

4. Nowhere do we find that Luz was not a Goth, or why Vitiza would invoke such a law, to say nothing of calling the inhabitants of the Iberian Peninsula *Spaniards* in the year 702.

5. Catálogo de las obras de Hartzenbusch. Novo y Colson, p. 411.

6. Obras, edición alemana, p. 6 of the prologue.

7. "History and legend in the plays of Juan Eugenio Hartzenbusch," unpublished thesis, Chapel Hill, 1970.

8. What power Alvar Fáñez has to dispose of the throne of Castile, especially offering it to a commoner, we are not told.

9. In scene seven Pilate implies that his wife, Procla, is related to Séneca: " . . . Filósofa, y al revés/ Hacer esta vez la cuenta/ De Séneca la parienta,/ Del gran Sabio cordobés."

10. Even assuming that Dimas was a child, how old is he, if Jesus was thirty-three? Dimas has not learned much good since.

Chapter Three

1. " . . . Hay equivocación lastimosa en creer que puede mancillar la memoria de alguien un hecho que se da por fingido . . . la mancilla, caso de haberla, recaería sobre el persona je vicioso, extendiéndose, cuanto más, a los que le dieron el ser y la educación, y que habiéndose cuidado de no poner apellido a la madre de Isabel, no puede haber familia que pierda nada por ese concepto."

2. Tirso de Molina wrote his play around 1614, but it was published much later. It is discussed in the chapter dealing with the Spanish classics.

3. Juan Pérez de Montalbán wrote his version of *Los Amantes de Teruel* at an uncertain date, but it was published in 1638 in the first volume of his plays, which bears the *aprobación* by Fray Gabriel Téllez dated 1635.

4. José Subirá. *El compositor Iriarte (1750–1791) y el cultivo español del melólogo.* Barcelona, 1949.

5. See note two, chapter four.

Chapter Four

1. The Comuneros' rebellious movement against the mandate of Carlos I, which placed foreigners in high government posts, was crushed in 1521, resulting in the execution of its leaders, Padilla, Bravo, and Maldonado.

2. "Yo, Comella, aquel fatal/ Comella, que daba a luz/ Un disparate mensual/ Para el Príncipe o la Cruz."

Chapter Five

1. Hartzenbusch doesn't mention that Lessing knew Spanish rather well and was acquainted with Lope de Vega's works.

2. Hartzenbusch doesn't explain why the daughter is going to die, or why the stepmother is responsible for her misfortune, and still less why she blesses her father, who chose the second wife the daughter curses.

3. "El fiscal./ Comprobando una copia/ Cierto señor fiscal impertinente,/ Púsose a corregir de mano propia/ Tres faltas que notó del escribiente,/ Descuidos ortográficos ligeros./ Raspó lo equivocado;/ Pero con tal desmaña o tal enfado,/ Que en el papel abrió tres agujeros;/ Y viéndolo inservible,/ Lo rasgó y lo tiró; barrió el criado,/ Y a un muladar lo echó, revuelto en broza./ Censor hay de genial tan apacible/ Que no ha de corregir si no destroza."

Chapter Seven

1. There is not a word about the stated date of 1696; it is obviously a mistake, since Tirso died in 1648 and could not have possibly mentioned events yet to come.

2. Hartzenbusch seems to have been inspired by this play he calls "disgusting" for his three pieces written for a child actress, in which very young girls express themselves in a language and with concepts beyond their years and demure character. See chapter two, part eleven.

3. An entry by Fr. Benito Remigio Noydens in the 1674 edition of the Covarrubias dictionary states that tobacco was discovered by the devil, and Pliny mentions it in his *Natural History*.

4. Indeed, since he became a monk in 1601.

5. Ordoño II, king of León from 914 to 924, lived before the *coplas de arte mayor*, the verse form referred to in the title, was in style.

6. Most cultured people know, as certainly do all Hispanists, that the legend of don Juan is found in ancient chronicles, and that, without a first dramatic version, others would not have followed the challenge to write about a dissolute young man who kicks a skull upon a lonely road, invites it to dinner, and then is surprised by the visit of the ghost to whom the skull belonged. Zamora had a different approach, but Don Juan is damned and cast into hell, as he is in Tirso's version. Also let us not forget that Tirso was a friar and that most of his daring plots contain moral teachings, sometimes very strong. Hartzenbusch's plots are usually far from original.

7. Hartzenbusch calls Zamora's version superior, but doesn't explain why. José Zorrilla was to make Don Juan really known, and his rendition of the theme, which maintains the first dare found in all versions, is still being performed traditionally in theaters throughout the Spanish-speaking world on November 1, All Saints Day (though television is taking over). Antonio Zamora's play was published in 1744.

8. In the facsimile, some of the words I find illegible, but enough of the Latin, and certainly the dates, can be made out to back the first part of Hartzenbusch's findings. Where he went wrong was in assuming, without a

shred of evidence to support his idea, that the other parts were also sent to the censor on the same date.

9. Even the Biblioteca Nacional of Madrid has no earlier edition than 1850, which leads me to believe that either it is very rare, a limited edition, or was not actually printed until 1850. It does not bear anywhere the indication that it may be a second edition, as Hartzenbusch's son states, nor is this point clear from subsequent printings, such as the seventh of 1924, or the 1944 without a number. A similar situation is found with the confusion of Lope de Vega's plays edited by Hartzenbusch, listed by people supposed to be trustworthy, as volume thirty-eight of the BAE; that particular volume contains plays by Lope de Vega, but the editor is Cayetano Rosell. Also, Hartzenbusch's son lists the fourth volume of Lope as forty-two, when in reality it is fifty-two. La Barrera is not much help here.

10. *Los Amantes de Teruel* is discussed in this chapter, as it was in chapter three.

11. "5. *Los amantes de Teruel.* —Representóla Avendaño.—Se incluye en esta colección, tan exactamente copiada, que hasta las erratas se han respetado. El Doctor Juan Pérez de Montalvan hizo una refundición de esta, que acaso sería ya refundición tambien" (p. xxxix).

12. Blanca de los Ríos proves this with a plate of the autograph manuscript between pages 866 and 867 of her own edition of Tirso plays, volume I, Aguilar, Madrid, 1946, which shows that the third part is dated August 1614. See also note 19, below.

13. Andrés Rey de Artieda wrote the first dramatic version of the historic legend of the Amantes in 1581, followed by Tirso's play. See chapter three for more information.

14. My master's thesis was a comparison of the three earliest dramatic versions of the legend of the Amantes and the one made by Hartzenbusch. The text of Rey de Artieda and Tirso de Molina's versions was published by me in *Taurus, Temas de España,* number 92.

15. Blanca de los Ríos, op. cit., pp. 128–129.

16. Barrera y Leirado, op. cit., p. 324. As stated, there is no such information in the 1850, 1924, or 1944 editions. See note 11.

17. There are a few *entremeses* and other short pieces included in volume four.

18. The list mentioned has caused scholars many a headache when trying to establish authorship of plays attributed to Calderón, because they are not in the list. Misreadings, variations in titles, and possible omissions are not considered by the purists.

19. I personally unscrambled the autograph manuscript of *La desdicha de la voz.* Professor Alva V. Ebersole made an edition based on said manuscript. (*Estudios de Hispanófila,* number 3, Valencia, 1963).

20. "Don Diego habla de las desdichas de Dorotea y del *daño* que la sigue, declarando que su fortuna *le ha enternecido*; sin embargo Dorotea nada le ha dicho. Harto será que no falte aquí una relacioncita."

21. He was a double hunchback.

22. On page 530, Corneille credits his *Menteur* (The Liar) to the Spanish play *La verdad sospechosa* (Suspicious Truth), which he copied in the belief that it was written by Lope de Vega. On page 531, Voltaire credits Spain for having inspired minds such as Corneille and Molière. Philarete Chasles takes several pages to prove the same point in an article dated 1847.

23. "El conde Lucanor, compuesto por el excelentísimo príncipe don Juan Manuel. Madrid, 1642." My objection is that Hartzenbusch is not merely quoting an edition, but the source, which should be dated accurately.

24. Aureliano Fernández Guerra. *Hartzenbusch, estudio biográfico y crítico* (Madrid, n.d.), p. 23.

25. Example: Pedro de Novo y Colson, *Autores dramáticos contemporáneos y joyas del teatro español del siglo XIX* (Madrid, 1881), p. 412. In the section dedicated to Hartzenbusch, the list of his works as published by Fernández Guerra is included.

26. Eugenio Maximino Hartzenbusch e Hiriart. *Bibliografía de Hartzenbusch* (Madrid, 1900), p. 429.

27. Pérez de Montalbán was a Godson of Lope de Vega, who had a great friendship with the former's father, a printer. His *Fama póstuma* (Posthumous Fame) is a eulogy of Lope on the occasion of his death, in 1635.

28. "La desdicha de la voz. Estrenada en setiembre de 1636," p. 589. See also note 19, above.

29. Ruiz de Alarcón's *Ganar amigos* (To Win Friends) and *Cautela contra cautela* (Caution Against Caution), which Hartzenbusch ascribes to Ruiz de Alarcón and Tirso de Molina, and the latter's *La romera de Santiago* (The Pilgrim Girl of Santiago).

30. See paragraph ending with note 16, above.

31. See notes 19 and 28, above.

32. See paragraph ending with note 29, above.

Chapter Eight

1. "Obras completas de Cervantes. Illustradas por los señores Don J. E. Hartzenbusch y Don Cayetano Rosell. Madrid. Imprenta de don Manuel Rivadeneyra. 1863."

2. Logic indicates that he could be the son of the first Cervantes, a nephew of the second, since the mother's last name, Saavedra, coincides in our author and Blas Cervantes, while Miguel de Cervantes's mother's surname could not possible be made to read Saavedra from either Cortinas or López. Also, the difference in age of the two children would make chronology rather awkward. Besides, a number of dictionaries, encyclopedias, and editions give Cervantes's birth year as 1547. These are a few examples, their information taken from older sources: *El pequeño Larousse ilustrado*, second edition, Paris, 1966. *Prontuario cronológico de historia de España*, Serie

Koel, No. 34, Tesoro, Madrid, 1964. In the end, this doubtful detail is immaterial.

3. Hartzenbusch must not have been too conversant with the fact that proofreading does not guarantee a perfect printing of one's own work.

4. In all fairness we must admit that photography was not popular at the time; however, there is a facsimile reproduction of a Tirso de Molina item in one of Hartzenbusch's works. See note eight, chapter seven, above.

5. Note 28. "Sucedió después de algún tiempo que los filisteos, juntando sus escuadrones para pelear, se reunieron en Socó y en Judá, y acamparon en los confines de Dommim. También se reunieron Saúl y los hijos de Israel, y viniendo al valle del Terebinto, ordenaron allí sus escuadrones para pelear contra los filisteos." L, Samuel, 17. "Goliat desafía a Israel." Sagrada Biblia, Félix Torres Amat, sexta edición. Apostolado de la Prensa, S. A. Madrid, 1965.

6. Note 38. "Le dí, traen las demás ediciones." "Vi, y no dí, escribiría Cervantes."

7. Note 234. Facsimile: "Figurósele que iba desnudo."

8. Note 5. "Aludiendose a la remedadora Eco, ninfa de tierra, no parece natural que Cervantes le aplicara el calificativo de húmeda, más propio de las ninfas de agua; tímida le convendría mejor, porque el eco habla siempre de lejos."

> "Eco, en otro tiempo ninfa, y por traidora
> a Juno, su señora, ...
> ....
> Mudóla en voz, que tímida responde
> del cóncavo lugar donde se esconde.

9. Note 143. "Se trata de rascarse, para lo cual hacen falta las manos, palabra que no está en las demás ediciones, y no sería por culpa del autor."

10. There is one on page two, two on pages five and seven, three on page eight, one on page fourteen, and one on page forty-two.

11. There seems to have been a text accompanying this edition, but I have not been able to find it, or a clear reference to it.

12. On page 109 there is a note of caution about three incomplete notes, only one identified by number. Why these notes were placed at the end of the series and not where they belong before the printing remains a mystery.

13. Note 37. "Cedí, en lugar de le di (cedí al Lazarillo la paja), sería más propio del caso, a nuestro entender." See note 6.

14. Note 388. See note 7.

15. Note 470. See note 8.

16. Note 1020. The facsímil reads: ". . . Quesi ahora me propusieran, y facilitaran un imposible, quisiera antes auerme hallado en aquella facción prodigiosa, que sano ahora de mis heridas, sin auerme hallado en ella. . . ."

Selected Bibliography

PRIMARY SOURCES

Primary sources are arranged chronologically (for a more complete listing of Hartzenbusch's works the reader is referred to chapter one, part three).

Ensayos poéticos y artículos en prosa literarios y de costumbres. Madrid: Yenes, 1843.

Obras escogidas. Prólogo de D. Eugenio de Ochoa. París: Baudry, 1850.

Obras escogidas. Edición alemana dirigida por el autor. Prólogo de D. Antonio Ferrer del Río. Leipzig: Brockhaus, 1863.

Obras. En colección de escritores castellanos líricos. Con la biografía del autor y juicio crítico de sus obras por D. Aureliano Fernández Guerra. Madrid: Tello, 1887.

Teatro escogido de Fray Gabriel Téllez, conocido con el nombre de El Maestro Tirso de Molina. Madrid: Yenes, 1839–1842.

Comedias de Don Pedro Calderón de la Barca. Madrid: BAE, 1848–1850.

Comedias escogidas de Fray Gabriel Téllez. Madrid: BAE, 1850.

Comedias de Don Juan Ruiz de Alarcón y Mendoza. Madrid: BAE, 1852.

Comedias escogidas de Frey Lope Félix de Vega Carpio. Madrid: BAE, 1853–1857.

"El Ingeniono Hidalgo Don Quijote de la Mancha", compuesto por Miguel de Cervantes Saavedra. Argamasilla de Alba: Rivadeneyra, 1863.

Las 1,633 notas puestas por el Excmo. é Ilmo. señor D. Juan Eugenio Hartzenbusch á la primera edición de "El ingenioso hidalgo." Barcelona: Ramírez y Cía, 1874.

SECONDARY SOURCES

ADAMS, NICHOLSON BARNEY. *Hartzenbusch's "Sancho Ortiz de las Roelas."* Reprinted from *Studies in Philology*, vol. XXVIII number 4, October 1931. This is a critique of the author's reworking of the play by that title by Candido María Trigueros, in turn a version of Lope de Vega's *La Estrella de Sevilla*.

ALCINA FRANCH, JUAN. *Teatro romántico*. Barcelona: Bruguera, 1968. Among other plays by Romantic authors, Alcina studies *Los Amantes de Teruel*, by Hartzenbusch.

BRETT, LEWIS E. *Nineteenth Century Spanish plays*. New York: Appleton-Century Crofts, Inc., 1935. A study of *Los Amantes de Teruel* with comments on the production of Hartzenbusch included. Contains a few errors.

145

CORBIÈRE, ANTHONY SYLVAIN. *Juan Eugenio Hartzenbusch and the French theater*. Thesis. Philadelphia, 1927. Better for the information it contains about Hartzenbusch and his times than for the author's viewpoint.

DE LOS RÍOS, BLANCA. *Fray Gabriel Téllez. Obras completas*, Tomo I. Madrid: Aguilar, 1946. Blanca de los Ríos points to inaccuracies found in Hartzenbusch's edition of Tirso's plays.

FERNÁNDEZ GUERRA, AURELIANO. *Hartzenbusch*. Estudio biográfico critico. Madrid: Imprenta de la Compañía de impresores y libreros, no date. A good source of some biographical material, as well as an appraisal of our author's works.

FERRER DEL RÍO, ANTONIO. *Galería de la literatura*. Madrid: Mellado, 1846. Among the portraits of several authors, there is a study on Hartzenbusch, the man and his works, by one who knew him for many years. Friendship doesn't prevent his being stern at times.

GARCÍA, SALVADOR. *Los Amantes de Teruel, de Juan Eugenio Hartzenbusch*. Madrid: Castalia, 1971. Repeats much material found in earlier editions of this particular play, aside from his own interpretation. The text is that of the original play, in five acts.

GIL DE ALBACETE, ALVARO. *J. E. Hartzenbusch. Los Amantes de Teruel. La jura en Santa Gadea*. Clásicos Castellanos, vol. 113. Madrid: Espasa-Calpe, 1954. The introduction, notes, and study of these two plays contain information found elsewhere as well about the author and his works.

HARTZENBUSCH E HIRIART, EUGENIO MAXIMINO. *Bibliografía de Hartzenbusch*, (Excmo. Sr. D. Juan Eugenio) formada por su hijo D. Eugenio Hartzenbusch. The most complete catalogue of Hartzenbusch's writings, including fragments of plays, unpublished material, and some erroneous information.

HEINERMANN, THEODOR. *Cecilia Böhl de Faber (Fernán Caballero) y Juan Eugenio Hartzenbusch*. Madrid: Espasa-Calpe, 1944. Although not concerning directly the works of Hartzenbusch this book contains biographical material not found in any other of the possible sources I have consulted.

Larra. Artículos de crítica literaria y artística. Edition by José Lomba y Pedraja. Clásicos Castellanos, vol. 52. Madrid: Espasa-Calpe, 1960. Among others, contains a critique of *Los Amantes de Teruel*.

NOVO Y COLSON, PEDRO DE. *Autores dramáticos contemporáneos y joyas del teatro español del siglo XIX*. Madrid: Fortanet, 1881. With a prologue by Antonio Cánovas del Castillo, this book is a most valuable source of information on the Romantic period as well as on the life and works of writers of the times.

Teatro Español. Teatro Español Borrás. These are collections of Spanish theater composed of individual editions of dramatic pieces of different periods. Collected in alphabetical order by author, *Teatro Español* contains plays by Hartzenbusch in volumes 140, 256, 257, and 258.

Teatro Español Borrás, volume 120, contains seven plays. The numbers given are those of the University of North Carolina collection, Chapel Hill.

UMPHREY, G. W. *Los Amantes de Teruel, por Juan Eugenio Hartzenbusch.* [Boston]: D. C. Heath and Co., 1920.

Other Reference Material

Excluding histories of literature and dictionaries, other books used in connection with the preparation of the present book to check, compare, clarify, or in some form complement information given by Hartzenbusch follow:

BARRERA Y LEIRADO, CAYETANO ALBERTO DE LA. *Catalogo bibliográfico y biográfico del teatro antiguo español.* Madrid: Rivadeneyra, 1860. Edición facsímil, Madrid: Gredos, 1969.

CERVANTES SAAVEDRA, MIGUEL. *El ingenioso hidalgo don Quijote de la Mancha.* Madrid: Cuesta, 1605, 1615. Edición facsímil, Palma de Mallorca: Alfaguara, The Hispanic Society of America y Papeles de Son Armadans, 1968.

COVARRUBIAS, SEBASTIÁN DE. *Tesoro de la lengua castellana.* Madrid: Luis Sánchez, 1611. Barcelona: S. A. Horta, 1943.

FLORES SETIÉN, ENRIQUE. *Memorias de las reinas católicas de España.* Madrid: Aguilar, 1945.

SERIE KOEL. *Prontuario cronológico de historia de España.* Madrid: Pueyo, 1941.

THOMAS, HENRY, trans. *The Star of Seville,* by Lope de Vega. London: Oxford Clarendon Press, 1930. Subsequently, London: Oxford University Press, 1950.

Index

(The works of Hartzenbusch are listed under his name)

148

DATE DUE